Improving Personal and Organisational Performance in Social Work

Improving Personal and Organisational Performance in Social Work

JANE HOLROYD

Series Editor: Keith Brown

Los Angeles | London | New Delhi
Singapore | Washington DC

www.learningmatters.co.uk

Los Angeles | London | New Delhi
Singapore | Washington DC

Learning Matters
An imprint of SAGE Publications Ltd
1 Oliver's Yard
55 City Road
London EC1Y 1SP

SAGE Publications Inc.
2455 Teller Road
Thousand Oaks, California 91320

SAGE Publications India Pvt Ltd
B 1/I 1 Mohan Cooperative Industrial Area
Mathura Road
New Delhi 110 044

SAGE Publications Asia-Pacific Pte Ltd
3 Church Street
#10-04 Samsung Hub
Singapore 049483

Editor: Luke Block
Development editor: Lauren Simpson
Production controller: Chris Marke
Project management: Swales & Willis Ltd,
Exeter, Devon
Marketing manager: Tamara Navaratnam
Cover design: Wendy Scott
Typeset by: Swales & Willis Ltd, Exeter, Devon
Printed by: MPG Books Group, Bodmin, Cornwall

Library of Congress Control Number: 2011945614

British Library Cataloguing in Publication Data

A catalogue record for this book is available from
the British Library

ISBN 978 1 44625 674 9
ISBN 978 0 85725 995 0 (pbk)

Contents

List of figures

List of tables

List of activities

Foreword

Never before has social work needed leadership development to ensure that every individual at every level is involved. The primary focus of this text is on self-leadership and concentrates on developing exquisite communication skills and resilience. In addition, the book aims to put you in the right frame of mind to make professional judgements based upon clarity of thought and depth of leadership awareness, to ensure that you are functioning at the very best of your capabilities.

It has been expertly produced by Jane Holroyd and is adapted from an earlier version co-written with Vicky Ross. It contains a wealth of clear advice and support regarding how best to improve personal and organisational performance. Jane's many years of experience are clear to see, and her expertise in leadership and management and the use of techniques such as neurolinguistic programming (NLP) provide a rich resource to all in social care or social work leadership.

It is my sincere belief that this text will benefit all who work in this field and, ultimately, their clients.

Professor Keith Brown
Series Editor
Director of Centre for Post Qualifying Social Work, Bournemouth University

About the author

Jane Holroyd has over 25 years' experience in the development and delivery of services within the NHS and was awarded an MBE for her achievements and services to nursing. She worked for the Leadership Centre where she was responsible for Medical and Nurse Director Leadership programmes and associated links with Europe. She co-authored the strategy document 'Leadership and Management Development for Social Work and Social Care – Creating Leadership Pathways of Progression' and also co-authored *Performance Coaching Skills for Social Work* (Sage). She is a specialist in developing leadership programmes and organisational development and is a public sector coach.

Acknowledgements

This book references many individuals within the fields of behavioural psychology and neurolinguistic programming, with particular mention to Richard Bandler and John Grinder. In addition, some of the text has been adapted from the original source (Holroyd and Ross, 2011 and Holroyd and Brown, 2011), and therefore my thanks go to Vicky Ross, Keith Brown and Bournemouth University.

Introduction

This book offers a radical service-oriented leadership approach for social work and care managers and is a deliberate move away from everything that has not worked before. It is outcome focused and solution centred and is an approach to explaining human behaviour, thought and communication in enhancing personal effectiveness and, ultimately, organisational performance. It is designed to support the development of aspiring and front-line managers in social work and care. The learning outcomes for this approach will focus on what truly matters and can be assessed against the National Occupational Standards for management and leadership (see Appendix 1).

Significantly, the information within is relevant, and equally useful, to health care and other public sector professionals. This book focuses on three key interrelated areas:

- self-leadership;
- resilience; and
- communication.

Fundamentally, mastering 'self-leadership' and becoming an exquisite communicator create resourcefulness, greater self-awareness, behavioural flexibility and effectiveness which manifests itself as innate resilience. This 'self-leadership' development centres on clear thinking (a focused mind), personal effectiveness and behavioural psychology and applies neuro-linguistic programming (NLP). The American co-founders of NLP were Richard Bandler, a scientist and mathematician, and John Grinder, a linguist.

Tosey's (2008) description of neurolinguistic programming refers to 'systemic links' between an individual's internal mental experience ('neuro'), language ('linguistic') and patterns of behaviour ('programming'). Walker (2004: 5) further describes the three components as:

- neuro – how we use our neurology to think and feel;
- linguistic – how we use language to influence others and ourselves;
- programming – how we act to achieve the goals that we set.

Representing a set of practical tools and techniques for thinking, behaving effectively and, ultimately, bringing out the best in people, NLP, suggest Singh and Abraham (2008: 146), 'gives managers and staff a quantum leap in the efficiency to work with, understand and motivate other people, both individually and in groups'.

NLP has been used with ever-growing veracity in the business world and is described as 'a collection of naturally occurring patterns of effective behaviour and communication that have been made explicit' (Tosey and Mathison, 2009: 15). According to the Chartered Institute of

Personnel and Development, NLP has become part of programmes in education, development, training in coaching, leadership development, management, communication, negotiating, cultural awareness, team building, personal advancement and many other applications to realise people's true potential (CIPD, 2008).

The approach set out in this book, therefore, has its roots in NLP and leadership development in order to provide a critical shift in effectiveness through changing the mindsets and behaviours of leaders and front-line staff not only to enhance personal effectiveness but also to bring about sustained team and organisational performance.

The NLP 'presuppositions' will be adopted as the guiding principles, values and standards throughout. Hayes (2008: 19) describes these 'as core attitudes and principles underpinning all approaches and techniques that NLP' has produced. These principles, according to Wake (2010: 17), were developed from an understanding of the beliefs of Milton Erickson (a medical hypnotherapist), Fritz Perls (the founder of Gestalt therapy) and Virginia Satir (a family therapist). Although not absolute truths, but more guiding standards or core principles, they provide a type of 'instinctive wisdom' (Alder, 1996: 24) fittingly applicable to these tools and techniques. See Appendix 2 for the list of the presuppositions.

The book is divided into four parts:

- **Part 1: Understanding thoughts and behaviours (Sections 1, 2, 3, 4, 5 and 6).** The principle introduced and emphasised is that everyone can be a leader, even if this is simply leading oneself effectively. 'Self-leadership', and why this is the focus throughout, is explained and defined. The impact of positive and negative thinking, and letting go of limiting thoughts, is examined in terms of enhancing self-awareness and personal self-management. Achieving successful thinking strategies and behaviours, understanding self, and how others may perceive you are also concepts explored in relation to personal leadership impact. The process and management of information through the five senses are discussed in relation to an individual's own internal filters. Emotional states and thoughts and how these thoughts affect behaviour are explored. The resultant language, and how purposefully changing such language can positively improve communication, is introduced. The ideology that we can reinvent ourselves by changing the way we think, and therefore fundamentally providing mental flexibility and psychological mobility, is a key component of this part.
- **Part 2: Becoming an exquisite communicator (Sections 7 and 8).** This part builds on the importance of understanding communication to be an exquisite communicator. Advanced non-verbal and verbal communication are therefore explored as two vital parts of a conversation. Understanding and recognising the impact of your own, and others', non-verbal communication are covered in detail. The concept of excellent rapport building and delivering the right message is discussed, together with how advanced questioning skills can reduce miscommunication, through eliciting what is often the hidden meaning behind the words and language patterns people use. How we can communicate more effectively and precisely to ensure that leaders are individually and organisationally more attuned is also explored.
- **Part 3: Effective influencing and motivating others (Sections 9 and 10).** Parts 3 and 4 are linked and explore the important constituent parts within sentences and language patterns which form the building blocks of human understanding. Part 3, in particular, centres on persuasive and motivational language in relation to understanding how individuals are motivated, process information and make decisions. The main focus is

positively influencing the behaviours of others through words that create results. Cross-boundary management and networking skills are critical to successful leadership. Leadership is about managing change rather than the status quo and, although the context can be described as important, the most significant facet is the relationships with people. This part of the programme, therefore, focuses on how to understand, motivate and influence others.

- **Part 4: Leading self (Sections 11, 12 and 13).** This final part links back to the first and the importance of 'self' and explores managing or redirecting limited thinking by identifying the purpose behind a belief and changing or reframing this for an individual. It examines techniques for reducing negative thoughts and feelings associated with an experience that is unhelpful and enhances positive and productive emotions linked to beneficial events or feelings. Developing greater flexibility in the way that individuals interact with their environment is, therefore, the main focus, with a clear emphasis on organisational and personal benefits. The methodology for setting explicit and achievable goals is incorporated to help individuals develop strategies to be more effective in everything they do. Identifying well-formed outcomes is therefore the focus. This final part integrates all that has been learnt from the previous sections. Managing 'self' through well-designed outcomes will be significantly impactful for the individual and the service they deliver in.

Overall intended learning outcomes

By the end of this book you will:

- have more choice over your style of leadership and understand where your similarities or differences are with individuals, your manager and stakeholders;
- be able to take responsibility for your own style of leadership and focus on how changing behaviours creates effective and sustainable change;
- acquire a better understanding of self in the professional context, creating and developing behavioural flexibility and resourcefulness in order to increase personal and professional effectiveness.

In addition you will:

- recognise and select strategies for improving communication and manage relationships more successfully with colleagues and the public;
- have flexibility in the choices you are able to make in your thinking and evaluate your own awareness of emotions in shaping performance, which will help to achieve and maintain effectiveness in managing self and the performance of others;
- create an awareness of your own and others' use of both enabling and inhibiting patterns in language and how to challenge these patterns to increase learning and change;
- be able to use advanced non-verbal communication and questioning skills to understand the meaning behind problems, which will allow you to deal with situations effortlessly;
- manage effective working partnerships with parents, carers, families and significant others;
- be able to excel in presenting, coaching, influencing and negotiating;
- deliver leadership for the organisation, provide direction to people, and enable, inspire, motivate and support individuals to achieve what the organisation has set out to do.

The intended learning outcomes and materials within this book meet the requirements and standards of the General Social Care Council leadership and management pathway. They have been developed in accordance with the Skills for Care Leadership and Management Strategy, the NHS Leadership and Qualities Framework (2004), and the NHS Knowledge and Skills Framework dimension, together with the functional areas identified as the National Occupational Standards for management and leadership. In addition, they satisfy the new Professional Capabilities Framework (PCF) and the Qualification Curriculum Framework Standards for Social Care Leadership and Management.

Part 1

Understanding thoughts and behaviours

Section 1
Starting with self

Braye (2002: 300) believes that 'leadership starts with self'. In this section, the concept of 'self-leadership' as something radical but simple, and something everybody is capable of, is proposed as a new paradigm of working from the 'inside out': of thinking and, therefore, behaving differently. The section focuses on the fundamental importance of communication (in its many different formats) and the way we interact with, and understand, each other. To become the very best we can be – professionally more effective and responsible as well as resilient role models and leaders – requires a look at 'self'.

Focusing on creating greater clarity in the moment impacts upon well-being and, therefore, productivity and creativity. This section examines popular approaches to leadership to explain why 'self-leadership' is the paradigm of choice for effective management, particularly with the current working backdrop and context.

The context

The complexity, ambiguity and pace of change in the health and social care public services are particular realities. The leadership environment therefore features some of the following daily challenges:

- emphasis on key performance indicators and a myriad of other targets;
- restructuring and cuts in public expenditure;
- increased management spans of control;
- functioning across boundaries with no line management accountability;
- dealing with multiple stakeholders;
- taxpayer scrutiny with political underpinnings;
- problems with recruiting and retaining the right staff;
- bureaucracy, with the resultant time pressures;
- information technology systems which do not interface with other systems;
- the extremes of human experience and behaviour;
- a high level of uncertainty about the right intervention, with risks in both not intervening and intervening;
- a shift in focus requiring more personalised solutions;
- ensuring that there is enough high-quality, evidence-informed support, with experience and expertise staying at the very interface of practice to supervise and develop the next generation of expert social workers;

- high-profile tragedies and cases, leading to micro-management and loss of both autonomy and, importantly, the artistry of professional judgement.

The above complexities require a leader who creates a questioning environment, listens and encourages others to listen and feel listened to, and promotes the right culture of developing and learning within the organisation. It requires a leader who asks the right questions, gathers all the information, uses questions to build teams, assesses the risks, manages conflict and handles difficult conversations, is organisationally aware, and looks to create independence in others. Principally, a leader is one who asks awkward questions and then listens, to co-create and shape strategy from the bottom, enabling effective and sustained change.

This type of leadership is not about a leader by title, who may be charismatic. It is not about systems, for we are all individually part of many systems. It is about every single individual and the individual's relationship with 'self'.

Why self-leadership?

A historical analysis demonstrates the shift in focus from the importance of characteristics and behaviours (invariably the 'great man' and 'trait' approaches) to the role of followers (transactional) and the context (contingency and situational) of leadership, to other examples, such as transformational leadership, which are outlined in Table 1.1.

Transactional approaches became synonymous with management, and transformational approaches synonymous with leadership, with Alimo-Metcalfe and Alban-Metcalfe (2005: 32) suggesting that transformational leadership is about 'enabling others to lead themselves'. Within the NHS, transformational leadership became the buzzword and represented the correct way to talk about and lead change.

The distinction between management and leadership has led to the concept that managers are people who 'do things right' (the what) and that leaders are people who 'do the right thing' (the how and why) (Bennis and Nanus, 1985: 221). However, in terms of reality, it is often one and the same person who fulfils both remits; the distinction not only creates an artificial permutation but also implies one role is better than the other.

Table 1.1 Leadership traits, theories and approaches

Great man theory	Leaders are exceptional and are born.
Trait theory	The emphasis is on a list of qualities leaders should have.
Behaviourist theories	The focus is on what leaders do – behaviours are categorised as 'styles of leadership'.
Situational leadership	Leadership is specific to the situation.
Contingency theory	This is a refinement of the situational approach, and involves identifying the situational variables which best predict the most effective leadership style.
Transactional leadership	The emphasis is on the leader and the follower, with rewards or recognition in return for commitment.
Transformational leadership	The central concept is change and the role of leadership in envisioning and transforming organisational performance.

Source: Bolden *et al.* (2003)

Table 1.2 Goleman's six leadership styles

1.	**Coercive**	Characterised by 'Do what I say.'
2.	**Authoritarian**	An approach which creates a vision and describes the overall goal(s).
3.	**Affiliative**	A style for building teams or increasing morale, with the suggestion that people come first.
4.	**Democratic**	Consensus developed through involving others, which can lead to endless meetings.
5.	**Pacesetting**	High performance standards set by the leader.
6.	**Coaching**	Focused on the development of others.

Transactional and transformational, however, remain a two-dimensional hypothesis, like autocratic versus democratic, and Avolio, Walumbwa and Weber (2009: 430) report that the evidence base for 'transformational leadership' trails 'behind all other areas of leadership research'.

Goleman (2000: 1) identified six styles of leadership in his study of executives, which are outlined in Table 1.2. While Goleman (2000: 1) would suggest using all six leadership styles to 'optimise business performance', the concept of diminishing complex interactions by switching between components of separate, and very distinct, styles could be perceived as inconsistent and confusing.

In Bolden *et al.*'s (2003) review of leadership theory and competency frameworks, the importance of the ability of the individual as a leader to listen is virtually missed by all the leadership frameworks examined. Interestingly, the concept of 'following' relating to a leader is not mentioned by any. Instead, there is an overwhelming and unmanageable list of attributes required of leaders in some of the models reviewed; one in particular unashamedly identified 83 characteristics from an original list of 1,013.

Leadership is not a function of personality, or traits that are exclusively inherited, or a style that can always be switched on in just the right way in a given situation or context. Grappling with the myriad of traits and behaviours, trying to understand leadership theory from a training course, or defining 'good' and 'outstanding' leadership behaviours (as though an individual only need copy these to become a 'great leader') makes no authentic, real or sustained sense.

An overreliance on competencies and standards distracts from the underpinning emphasis within this text: the importance of the process of developing and adapting to become something more 'real'. Leadership in this context, however, is about more than simply being a leader by title and position.

Position and post holder

Leadership has been perceived in the past to be the 'gift' and remit of the post and title holder. Many still think of leadership in terms of positional power. The expectations on such individuals are almost superhuman, with some of these described by Bolden *et al.*:

He/she is seen to act as an energiser, catalyst and visionary equipped with a set of tools (communication, problem solving, people management, decision making etc.) that can be applied across a diverse range of situations and contexts ... excellent information processing, project management, customer service and delivery skills, along with proven business and political acumen, building partnerships, walk the talk, show incredible drive and enthusiasm and get things done . . . whilst the leader demonstrates innovation, creativity and thinks 'outside the box' . . . they like to be challenged and they're prepared to take risks . . . honesty, integrity, empathy, trust, ethics and valuing diversity are added to the list.

(2003: 37)

Reliance on individual positions potentially sets up the person and the organisation to fail, especially with the flattening of structures, where individual accountability can become lost in the vast spans of responsibility; this concept, therefore, no longer fits. Ensuring every single individual counts and concentrating on self as the leadership focus are characteristic of a 'dispersed leadership' approach, which becomes the vehicle for creating a momentum of significant and sustained cultural change. Katzenbach and Smith (1993: 45) describe 'dispersed leadership' as: 'people with complementary skills who are committed to a common performance purpose, performance goals, and approach for which they hold themselves mutually accountable'. Engaging expertise collaboratively within the organisation rather than concentrating on formal remits is proposed to increase professional responsibilities, add to a learning culture and create better teamwork (Hafford-Letchfield, 2007).

Borrowed models

Some models, methodologies and approaches have been borrowed from 'elsewhere' and are seen as the next ideal thing to learn and follow. The public sector, for example, has looked to the construction industry in the shape of PRINCE II (PRojects IN Controlled Environments), although it fits poorly with the true requirements of social work and care. Lean and Six Sigma (www.leansigma.com/index.php), borrowed from business, have transferable qualities to inform more efficient ways of working. However, social work and care provision is about much more than efficient work habits.

Additional models of leadership development have been introduced from outside in the belief that someone else has all the answers. The typical example for the NHS was the 'Leading an Empowered Organisation' (LEO) approach, imported from the United States, which, while having a brief impact, became another training course to add to the suitcase. Other models, approaches and ideal behaviours proposed as the latest in leadership development include the case for the authentic leader.

Authentic leadership

Understanding self in the fullest sense – what motivates an individual and is the individual's true passion – is essential to discovering purpose (Bass and Steidlmeier, 1999). Discussions about the lack of authenticity within corporate leadership seem to have resulted in the need to specify and propose an approach based on 'acting with integrity' (Kouzes and Posner, 2007: 50) and finding one's values. The model has been described by a number of authors; Sparrow (2005: 422), for example, alludes to 'consistency', which he believes results from 'self-awareness' and 'self-regulation'.

Avolio, Walumbwa and Weber (2009: 424) describe four features, which include 'self-awareness' and three other dimensions:

1. 'balanced processing', for example objectively analysing before deciding;
2. 'internalised moral perspective': being guided by internal ethical standards;
3. 'relational transparency': being open and sharing.

Others have mentioned 'self-sacrifice', 'spirituality', 'ethical leadership' and 'authentic behaviours' (Gardner *et al.*, 2005; Klenke, 2005). Sparrow (2005: 421), however, stresses that this process is not advanced independent of exchange, but requires 'ongoing clarification' that can only be provided by others.

The ethical or moral facet seems to presuppose that if you are not 'authentic' you are 'inauthentic'. This two-dimensional aspect of either/or arguably fits the criticism levelled at other bipolar spectrum models, for example transactional and transformational, or democratic and autocratic, which were mentioned earlier.

However, each of the authors above mentions two constructs which are both mutual to 'self-leadership': self-awareness and self-regulation. Sparrow (2005: 436) also importantly alludes to the process of development, which is a central feature of 'self-leadership'.

Self-leadership – a new approach

The leadership development focus within this book is based on fundamental principles related to 'self-leadership' and 'inside-out understanding'. It concentrates on creating and delivering behavioural change, which can be evidenced within the practical, 'real' world of front-line service delivery. Significantly, it is an instinctive model and approach which is easily transferable and promoted with service users. It is a methodology for creating choices from what can often seem like no options, fundamentally to teach individuals how to see and learn to create their own choices, together with a greater flexibility and independence of thought. It creates the option of responsibility and accountability while improving well-being and resilience.

It is:

- a way to tap into the human spirit to create constructive change;
- a way to bring out the best in people;
- a way to move people to well-being and away from problems;
- a way to draw out internal resilience;
- a way to prevent community problems from the inside out.

(Pransky, 2003)

What is self-leadership?

Self-leadership has been defined as 'the process of influencing oneself' to create the direction and motivation needed to perform (Neck and Manz, 2009: 4). The concept of 'self' is closely related to the important facet of self-awareness, defined by Goleman (2000: 4) as 'the ability to read and understand your emotions as well as recognize their impact on work performance, relationships and the like'. 'Self'-leadership, however, is also linked to the above notion of 'dispersed leadership', which focuses on 'self-management'.

However, self-leadership is more than the self-management which is linked with the individual equally managing as a form of distributed or dispersed leadership; it is about changing individual behaviour as a result of changing the way someone thinks. It is the concept that we cannot control everything, but we can control our reaction to a situation. The notion of thoughts and how we think influences the chemical responses which create emotional feelings and resultant behaviours, in terms of action and reaction. What we are thinking therefore affects the way we feel and behave and is the foundation of habits. Thinking differently is a focus throughout.

It is about changing the faulty thinking strategies that individuals have grown up with and the unproductive states they produce, for example of over-analysing, negative thinking, low confidence and self-doubt. It concentrates on the leadership quality of a clear mind and the prime importance of communication.

Self-leadership involves, as Neck and Manz (2009: 4) describe, 'leading oneself' using both behavioural and cognitive strategies to influence personal effectiveness positively. Behavioural strategies are those of self-observation and include 'self-goal setting', 'self-reward' and 'self-cueing'; the cognitive strategies incorporate examining internal dialogue, beliefs and assumptions.

'Self-observation' encompasses the information an individual has about the self: what the individual is aware of. The process of evaluating 'self' in different situations provides additional information about the conditions in which certain behaviour is manifested. For example, individuals may notice or observe what stops them writing a report they know should have been completed.

'Self-goal setting' includes all the actions which are purposefully taken in an effort to achieve a predetermined outcome. Arguably, individuals function for a significant part of their lives without consciously concentrating their efforts on exactly what they are going to achieve. Self-goal setting may, for example, be about identifying specific behaviours which individuals want to enhance or decrease.

'Self-reward' includes creating incentives for an identified outcome. It could be manifested, for example, by establishing rewards for the completion of different tasks.

'Self-cueing', for Neck and Manz (2009: 16), would involve identifying and 'increasing positive cues' or prompts to take certain action, for example producing a list or purposefully working in an environment which prompts the right behaviours to achieve a task effectively.

The significance of focusing on creating leadership of a clear mind, awareness and the importance of communication, however, distinguishes Neck and Manz's (2009) concept of self-leadership from the model of self-leadership proposed in this text. Communication is made up of written, verbal and non-verbal interactions; arguably, these are the only ways to interact with the world.

This is not about leadership being simply about self; it also encompasses how an individual with self-leadership works more effectively within teams, organisations and, fundamentally, all interactions. It is about changing behaviour as a result of transforming the way people think and what they are paying attention to. Leading projects or work without the reciprocal authority (or without the required authority) is a good example of how self-leadership and the ability to influence others with intentional communication can create effective and sustainable partnerships based on successful relationships.

Uniquely, however, 'the only person we can continually inspire, prod and shape – with any degree of success – is the person in the mirror' (Patterson *et al.*, 2002: 29). In essence, no one can really change how individuals do something other than the individuals themselves, and as everything we do is based upon thoughts and thinking, which invariably create actions and reactions, the nearest step to changing individuals' behaviour is to help them to change their thinking.

To improve people's performance starts with getting the individuals to change their thoughts, to motivate if motivation is the issue or to change their thinking if lack of confidence or self-belief is paralysing them. Becoming more 'self-aware' helps individuals to tune into their 'own style' – their unique way of thinking, as Neill (2009: 176) describes it – and to understand their 'unconscious assumptions, filters and habits' and how they impact on others.

Neill (2009) contends that we will almost always see and hear what we are looking for: listening out to confirm our beliefs and assumptions and, in so doing, delicately creating the world as we perceive it to be – this is something which will be revisited. The building blocks of change are fundamentally about developing an awareness of our behaviours and the attributing factors. The important link here is the quality of thinking, moving from a 'victim mentality' to a mindset of responsibility and of taking control and with it a resilience, creativity and collaborative focus.

Developing this insight is not simply about switching it on as you walk into work, for home life stresses 'bleed' into the working day no matter how professional individuals believe they are. In 'overworked environments' (the builder of chronic stress) the evidence seeps out and shows its hand, at the very least in non-verbal clues.

This 'principle-based' approach is considered an 'inside out model of psychological functioning, meaning one's thoughts determine one's sensory experience, which in turn create one's personal reality and experience of external life circumstances' and therefore prima facie the starting point (Roy, 2007: 195). The quality of mind, thinking and awareness therefore becomes the leadership focus to create the required insight in the moment, to transform reactions and actions and to ensure decisions made are from the right state of mind.

The premise throughout this book is that anyone can be a leader; even those who do not manage others still have to manage and lead themselves (Hock, 2002). As Kouzes and Posner (2007: 337) state, 'leadership is everyone's business'. It is about self-realisation and trans-formation, recognising our strengths and weaknesses, and developing to become the best that we can be. It starts with individual change. Blanchard (2007: 101) describes self-leadership as integral to 'effective leadership' and that 'before you can hope to lead anyone else, you have to know yourself . . . self-knowledge provides perspective'.

Senge *et al.* (1999: 195) would describe this as 'personal mastery'. This is a unique individual journey that is developed over time and with knowledge, experience and maturity. What is learnt in the classroom or from a book will not have as much value until it is applied in practice. Acquiring true knowledge and understanding of self and how we behave is an ongoing process where learning is converted into action and practised.

The next step is to shift the focus from self to others, and that can happen effectively only when there is an objective understanding of thinking, thought creation and the outcome being the process of behaviour (Dispenza, 2007). When it is recognised how resourceful or unresourceful states are created, individuals can then observe someone else's, adopt the attitude of curiosity and notice what processes the other person is engaged in to create the behaviour. 'Resourceful' in this context denotes the conscious ability to elicit the most appropriate disposition or psychological state matched to achieve whatever is required for that occasion. The 'state' is the behavioural expression; worried, anxious, happy and excited are examples. Recognising that one is in an unresourceful state can paralyse creativity and an individual's resolve.

In understanding the process of behaviour we equip ourselves with an appreciation of someone else's world, and that person's motivational drivers, limitations and resources. It is only then that we are able to help someone reach his or her aspirations and full potential.

Developing thoughts and thinking

According to Kouzes and Posner, 'To find your voice you have to explore your inner territory' (2007: 50). The development of leadership therefore starts with knowledge and an understanding of self and how individuals construct the world in which they live. When human beings see, hear or feel something for the first time, they have no internal reference to what this might be. In time, the repetition of all experiences builds internal references, and memories are developed. Through learning in this way individuals can name something and create meaning. This labelling process occurs where tangible objects are given significance; this activity grows to include experiences (Dispenza, 2007). In this way past memories are accessed with specific emotions, even if these may actually be unhelpful.

As a person matures, this process diminishes as the environment becomes more and more familiar. This progression helps individuals to become efficient, as they no longer need to learn everything as they see it. The world, in simple terms, becomes predictable; if they do the same thing, nothing new is learnt. This predictability means that the environment causes a reactive thinking. However, if the environment does not change, a person does not evolve. The environment can progress and develop only from a thought that is created about something that does not exist in the environment; learning and development ensue, and the cycle begins again (Dispenza, 2007).

Everything that can be seen once did not exist; it was a thought that was created internally in the mind and then recreated externally by sharing with others. A fundamental question Kehoe (2010) would ask is: are you going to live your life through the creation of others, or are you working to evolve yourself and create a world that inspires and motivates you, to achieve all your ambitions?

True leadership is recognising what is lacking and how things can change and improve. It is about using imagination to find out what is missing and discover how it can be initiated. Sometimes the things that individuals create have been modelled by others, so the inspiration may be someone else's; however, the outcome is still unique to each person, and so we have truly evolved.

Senge *et al.* (1999) would report that individuals evolve themselves and, as a result, they develop the environment that they influence, and yet it is much more than simple 'personal mastery'; it is about the 'how', and understanding that we can change our thoughts and within the clarity of the moment create a leadership wisdom that matters and makes the difference.

ACTIVITY **1.1**

Leadership characteristics

List ten qualities that, in your opinion, are characteristics of good leaders.

- *Rate yourself out of ten for each quality, with ten being the highest and zero being the lowest.*
- *Notice what you perceive to be important and note your score. For each, identify what you have to do to increase the number.*

TIPS FOR SUCCESS

- *It is important to start with 'self'; going there first is a fundamental principle of true leadership.*
- *Be more than simply 'self-aware' to create a deeper appreciation of how an individual acts and reacts in the moment. This awareness creates the flexibility to be more resourceful.*
- *The process of influencing 'self' as a focus to perform better is fundamental to your personal and wider organisational effectiveness.*
- *Build clarity of mind through 'self-leadership' to enhance creativity and also provide the conduit for better decision making.*

Section 2

How to understand our thoughts

In Section 1 there was a brief introduction to developing thoughts and thinking and acknow-
ledgement of how new information is processed and becomes cognitive routine. Although
both sides of the brain are used, the right tends to be involved in processing 'new' or novel
information and the left with standard operating or routines. This section focuses on how
further to understand thoughts and thinking processes. This knowledge will provide the
building blocks to understanding behaviour.

There have been significant advances in neuroscience, particularly with modern imaging
equipment – magnetic resonance imaging (MRI) and positron emission tomography (PET) scans
– which is revealing new understandings about the brain, typically the degree of plasticity or
neuroplasticity. This is the ability of the brain to adapt both structurally and cognitively. For
example, for many years it was believed that all human beings had a finite number of brain
cells and lost plasticity as they became adults. New evidence suggests this is not the case, and
the plasticity continues 'well into adulthood and possibly throughout the lifespan' according to
Goldberg (2009: 234).

Other advances include the detection of 'mirror neurones', which 'are cells whose activity
reflect their surrounding' (Medina, 2008: 269). Work with primates revealed that the same
pattern of brain activity occurred regardless of whether they observed another monkey picking up
a raisin or physically completed the action themselves. These cells are responsible for imitating.

However, what does this all mean in relation to leadership? From a physiological perspective
the brain is exceptionally adaptive and capable of so much; indeed it has an extraordinary
'compensating' capacity (Goldberg, 2009: 235). It is accepted that individuals 'constantly
reconfigure and re-associate' information, which is evidenced within the neural networks
(Goldberg, 2009: 235). Leading, therefore, is about knowing how to move forward and to
make the required changes to support individuals within an organisation in the way that they
need to be encouraged. It is about changing behaviour as a result of transforming the way
people think and what they pay attention to.

However, before change can be realised the starting point is 'self' and understanding
thought processes. To achieve this, a 'leader' must first understand how individuals' thoughts
influence all that they do. The way thinking creates a 'perceived reality' is a fundamental
concept and principle that we will focus on throughout. Being preoccupied with thoughts of
worry, for example, stops individuals being clear in the now.

An individual experiences approximately 60,000 thoughts per day. However, not all of these
capture the attention; there is an unconscious selection process running in the background. The
most significant decision is deciding what is important, for then a thought gains prominence.

What most people are not aware of is that they have a choice whether to hold on to a thought or declare it unproductive and let go of it.

Dispenza (2007) describes how focusing and placing our attention on pain in the body can actually produce the sensation of pain and, conversely, changing our attention can stop the process. He describes this mechanism of directing attention as one that brings 'everything to life and makes real what was previously unnoticed or unreal' (Dispenza, 2007: 3). Every thought therefore, whether intentional or not, creates 'a cascade of chemical reactions that produce not only what we feel but also how we feel' (Dispenza, 2007: 2).

Every action has a reaction and therefore a result. Take the example of someone who stays up late to complete a paper on the night before a deadline because other work had up till then been considered more urgent or because working with colleagues on different agendas had been deemed more important. These responses result in the individual staying up very late to produce the paper on time.

Examining the specifics of each action taken rather than the result or outcome is an important starting point in creating change. If the actions or reactions were to be further examined it would become clear that they are not simply spontaneous. Feelings are always linked to an action, so in our example what feelings were experienced which stimulated avoidance and created the resultant late work on the paper? Was there a lack of motivation? Was the person nervous, apprehensive, irritated or upset? Maybe there is another explanation? Emotions are not haphazard; instead, they are the result of feelings being activated, which in turn create the motivation which produces an outcome.

If individuals intend to learn something new, their attention will be on noticing what is different, for the mind is predisposed to spotting new details or differences as part of the process of learning. This 'intention' to learn determines what the individuals pay attention to. How individuals determine what is significant or not is linked to the beliefs and values learnt from the day they were born. Parents and society have played a crucial part, flavoured by experiences from life, producing an individual tapestry of beliefs and values.

If this were to be reduced even further, the thought becomes the component part (see Figure 2.1). What was the person thinking at the time that caused the feeling, which created an action that had a specific result?

What would happen if the thought was altered? Would that in turn change the feeling? If the feeling was different, would it create a different action and, therefore, a different result?

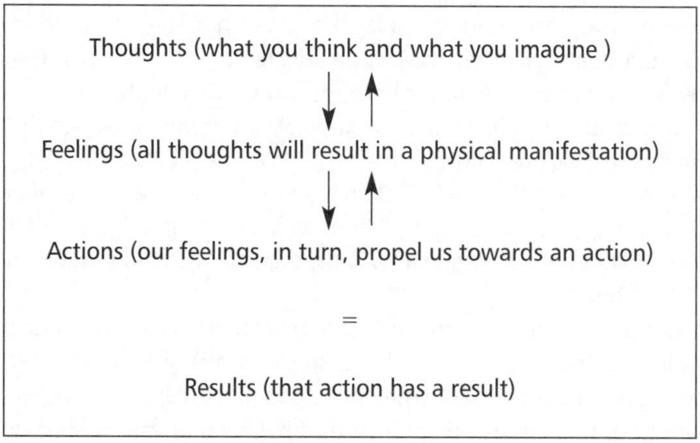

Thoughts (what you think and what you imagine)

↓ ↑

Feelings (all thoughts will result in a physical manifestation)

↓ ↑

Actions (our feelings, in turn, propel us towards an action)

=

Results (that action has a result)

Figure 2.1
Turning thoughts
into actions

Positive change occurs when individuals become aware of their thoughts and decide to stop doing what they may have routinely done in the past, making changes to their thoughts in the present moment. This has a reciprocal response; it will result in a different feeling, motivating a different action, and creating a different result.

Having the courage to do something distinctive to challenge one's own status quo, to identify new ways of doing things, is integral to being an effective leader of 'self' and others. It is beyond being 'brave'; it is about tapping into something more profound, which is instinctive and based on innate wisdom.

We can look at the process in Figure 2.1 from the thoughts that result in a feeling that motivates us to an action that has a result. Alternatively, you can look at the result and ask yourself: what were the actions? What feelings did I have that motivated me towards that action? What was I thinking that created that feeling (Holroyd and Ross, 2011: 10)?

This important concept is stressed by Bandler (2008a, 2008b) and Dispenza (2007): that by changing thoughts a chemical reaction ensues which quite literally 'changes' an individual's mind. Therefore 'what' and 'how' individuals habitually think, or focus their attention on, are what they neurologically create inside and what essentially they become and demonstrate. This is captured succinctly in the following quote by Alder and Heather: 'What most occupies your mind, whether intentionally or unintentionally, tends to turn into behaviour and reality' (1998: 19).

Changing thoughts and thinking

While it is accepted that new knowledge and information are continually integrated, by specifically what mechanism ('how' it is 'preserved'), especially when there is a continuous adaptive process, is not known (Goldberg, 2009: 235). What is known, however, is that individuals are able to influence their own thoughts and thinking (Sedgeman, 2005).

'What we see is what we get' (Pransky, 2003: 85) describes how people in the same desperate circumstances can express a completely different perspective. These are categorised in Figure 2.2. The bottom of the pyramid denotes individuals who get caught up in life, and Pransky suggests that people who 'cause harm to themselves and others' would be in this grouping. The second, 'stuck', category would include the 'teenager who believes she needs a baby to make her life whole'. The third group is where probably most people reside, individuals who move in and out of stressful events, with those at the lower end in difficult roles or marriages. People in the fourth group are more at ease; they see 'that their actions are generated internally' and know that they decide whether to be affected or not by events. They 'tend not to dwell on problems' and know they 'don't have to take personally the results of other people's thinking'. The final category is the 'wise and extremely insightful'; they 'see that their thoughts are the only reality they will ever know'.

Pransky (2003: 86) suggests that individuals 'think, feel and act out of whichever way they see life', depicted by the pyramid in Figure 2.2. He cites Banks, who states that: 'The wisdom humanity seeks lies within the consciousness of all human beings, trapped and held prisoner by their own individual minds' (2003: 87).

This is about changing thoughts, moving away from a 'victim mentality' to look within and to accept individual responsibility for the perceived world, our so-called reality. It is not about positive thinking but acknowledging in the moment whether a thought is helpful or not and what an alternative view might be. It is about acceptance that beliefs and values, held so

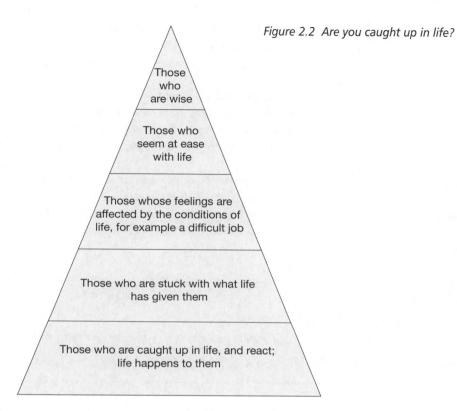

Figure 2.2 Are you caught up in life?

strongly, are simply guiding maps used to make sense of the world, and, while they may have been useful to us as children, they may no longer be as helpful. The important acceptance is that thoughts are 'fleeting'; whether an individual holds on to them and ruminates is a matter of choice. This is not about selecting and keeping only the so-called positive thoughts, but about which ones we give our attention to.

It is not about techniques as such but acceptance of a different way of thinking, about stripping back the 'filters' (developed as internal rules, principles, standards, values and beliefs) and being more aware in the moment. It is about breaking thinking habits. Ironically, this is something that can be implemented straight away, remembering the benefits of an unconstrained creative potential.

Organisations, as human constructs, can also become stymied by unproductive thinking.

Organisations and change

Classically, the repetition of doing things, because they have always been done in a particular way, becomes easily imprinted within the minds of organisations and the individuals who work in them. Like unchallenged thoughts, they become habits and daily behaviours. Indeed, Morgan (2006) uses the metaphor of 'the brain' to describe an organisational form. Unlike other complex organisations made up of many people, individuals can more easily change their thoughts and build new beliefs, and in turn demonstrate new behaviours.

One of the greatest flaws of organisations is that they spend an incredible amount of energy and funds on redesigning services following the latest tools, techniques or methodologies, and create policies and procedures which few staff have fully integrated in their daily practice because, operationally, there is a mismatch and staff do not truly own or engage with them. Forcing individuals through this so-called 'change funnel' process creates well-recognised organisational resistance and failure.

Instead, start with 'self' and support individuals to understand the nature of their thoughts and thinking and the impact of being in the best possible state, instinctively resilient and receptive to change. This creates individuals who are more able to challenge appropriately (where challenge is required) and in essence are more behaviourally receptive to the change process.

Being receptive to, and further developing, experiential wisdom is an innate potential within all staff, providing they can quieten their minds to listen. Implicitly, being able to tune into the ability to perceive what is crucial and important in a given operational work situation combines unique intelligence with evidence and experienced know-how. This is about real change from the inside.

ACTIVITY **2.1**

Results you want to change

Think about a result you want to change, something you may wish you had done differently.

- *What action occurred to create the result and what was the feeling you had at the time?*

TIPS FOR SUCCESS

- *Creating clarity of thought will help you as a manager and leader to improve your decision-making processes.*
- *Changing unhelpful thoughts and thinking creates possibilities previously stifled and therefore increases the potential level of effectiveness.*
- *Clarity of thought has an infectious response, something which provides an added dimension to role modelling.*

Section 3
The process of behaviour

This section examines the process of behaviour and building self-awareness.

Leadership is not about personality; it's about behavior.

(Kouzes and Posner, 2007: 15)

Behaviour has been described as the specific physical actions and reactions through which we interact with people and the environment around us (Molden, 2007). Others, for example Dompke (2001: 11), have suggested that observed differences in human behaviour are related to the person's characteristics, the situation and the interplay: 'it is a change from one state to another state (bodily and/or mentally); is always goal-oriented; is a reaction to an external observable stimulus or to an internal covert stimulus; and has three interrelated components – a cognitive, a psycho-motor and a socio-affective component'.

The rational planning mind exists in the frontal lobe of the brain, the area above the eyes and behind the forehead. This part is responsible for how we interrelate with the world and perceive reality, and how we can achieve further than our genetical predisposition, learn from our mistakes and choose to behave in the moment. We have the capacity to think, rationalise and have a conscience; however, the one thing in life that is not taught is how to think and appreciate fully our thinking.

Thinking is one thing that differentiates us all. The default position of unconscious living, with the concept that the external environment dictates and controls what happens, negates the choice that really exists, which is to take back the internal control of thinking and thoughts.

In Section 2 we discussed the concept of actions and reactions being the result of a feeling which was stimulated by a thought. All behaviours can be reduced to these three components (see Figure 2.1). There is a thought and, at the moment the thought is created, a physical manifestation is produced, along with an internal dialogue or self-talk.

The thought is therefore first; for example, thinking about a past time when we were angry can reproduce the feelings experienced at the time. This could manifest itself as an instant physical tension in the neck, shoulders and jaw area; the breathing may become shallow, and possibly the fists will be clenched and facial muscles pulled forward and downwards, causing the brow to furrow. The brain does not differentiate between real and remembered stimuli, for it has been shown that the identical neurons are activated in the same part of the brain. As a result, the physical response has just as much impact, as though reliving the experience (Benedict, 2008).

At the same time there is an internal dialogue running inside the head, which is passing comments about the event. All individuals have an internal dialogue, or 'self-talk' (Bandler, 2008b: 80), even if they are totally unaware of it most of the time.

Behaviour is manifested internally through the production of chemicals and hormones and the impact on the body's physiology and neurology (unconsciously), and externally denoted by the 'state', the emotional visible expression. Managing one's state is described as an important behavioural flexibility which can greatly improve an individual's performance (Wake, 2010). Behavioural flexibility is the proficiency in adapting an outwardly verifiable response to different requirements and situations.

Varying your behaviour rather than approaching and doing more of what has not worked in the past is a good example. By understanding the process of behaviour an individual can start to build flexibility and, in doing so, creates greater choices. Achieving behavioural flexibility is the aim, although most behaviour in the right context is useful.

Questions to ask with an attitude of curiosity (being the observer rather than the judge) are:

- Is what I am thinking true?
- What evidence do I have that it is true?

To understand from a physiological perspective how to make changes, the following questions are useful:

- What is happening in my body?
- How am I reacting?
- What is my body telling me?

Deciding in the moment what can be changed purposefully, for example changing the breathing pattern, will create a different feeling, a change in 'biochemical output' (Dispenza, (2007: 43). Relaxing tense muscles will also produce a physiological change.

This mind–body connection is evident, so, when an individual is focused on a perceived intractable problem, the outward physical manifestation will match or be congruent and, therefore, visibly aligned. According to Dispenza (2007: 305) there are seven primitive emotions:

- anger;
- surprise;
- joy;
- sadness;
- disgust;
- contempt;
- fear.

Furthermore, all experiences an individual has would include a combination of the above basic emotions. These emotions are identified as visible verbal clues and are discussed further in Section 7 in relation to Ekman's (2003) work on universal facial expressions.

Emotions can be experienced in the moment and are potentially fleeting; 'moods', however, can last longer and provide the underlying backdrop or 'filter'. Cheal (2010: 28) suggests that this 'background mood' creates a tendency to be predisposed or 'primed', and provides the example of someone in 'an irritable mood' being easily inclined to the emotion of anger. This is further compounded, he suggests, by the 'emotion' creating the propensity in an individual to find reinforcements in the external world to confirm the feelings in a 'looping and self-fulfilling prophecy', wheel or 'mood loop' (Cheal, 2010: 29). Neill advocates that: 'Your day doesn't create your mood; your mood creates your day' (2009: 124). Roy advises that 'emotions are the result of thought, and conflicts result from thought, as do resistance, defences and problems' (2007: 196). Emotions, however, 'get our attention'; the more significant they are, the more they are remembered (Medina, 2008: 79). They are the reaction individuals have to their own thoughts.

Dispenza (2007: 46) describes the process of unconscious ways of thinking and conscious thoughts producing chemical reactions, which lead to a behaviour, the repetition of which creates 'acquired patterns of behaviour that are almost involuntary . . . and neurologically hardwired in the brain'. Although the patterns are described as 'hardwired', Dispenza (2007: 175) advocates that we can reinvent ourselves by literally changing our thinking.

If the physical demeanour is changed by smiling and the thoughts replaced by recalling a happy event, this will change how someone feels. Reflecting on a problem which may previously have preoccupied an individual while in the above 'happy state' may produce a wholly different perspective and outlook. Importantly, as Pransky (2003: 183) stresses, before attempting to do anything with anyone – providing information, explaining, teaching, presenting, eliciting information – it is vital to 'be in a good feeling in that moment'.

This behavioural flexibility links to the concept of 'situational leadership' (the Hersey-Blanchard model originally developed in 1969 and cited in Blanchard, 2007) and matching behaviour to what is perceived to be required. However, increasing the knowledge of how behaviour is produced and, most importantly, how an individual responds to certain stimuli, with this higher awareness in the moment and the choice it creates, is different, and distinct, from simply learning a set of prescribed leadership competencies or responses. It is arguably something more real and integral to 'self' as opposed to wearing something specified and therefore potentially artificial.

Understanding the above processes is important in managing first 'self' and then others. Building self-awareness through appreciating the basics of behaviour and the conceptual building blocks is an important part of developing as a leader. Figure 3.1 shows the component parts as identified above: there is a thought, which creates a neurochemical-induced feeling (a physical manifestation), with outward verification in the form of behaviour and non-verbal evidence, and at the same time there is 'self-talk' or internal dialogue, for the body is governed by what the mind tells it to do.

An example to illustrate the above further would be an individual who is presenting to a group of key stakeholders or who is making a court appearance; the individual is thinking that he or she is no good at presenting and creates pictures in his or her head of previously recollected bad experiences or predictive images of what could happen. This is manifested in the 'self-talk', for example 'I'm no good at this', 'It's all going to go wrong again', 'Why do I always feel like this?' or 'Why can't I be like other, confident people?' The feelings reveal themselves as a sick sensation or butterflies, and the outward display is of someone who may be biting his or her bottom lip, breathing rapidly in the upper chest, or looking pale and generally uncomfortable and anxious.

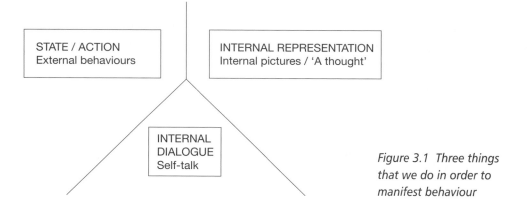

Figure 3.1 *Three things that we do in order to manifest behaviour*

Importantly, we learn to do something and then this learning becomes unconscious, so we are able to do things without thinking. As a result, actions become automatic and easy because regular routines become hardwired neural networks (Dispenza, 2007). In order to change our behaviours, we need to become consciously aware, understand the step-by-step processes which created the behaviour, and then make relevant changes.

By changing thought processes, individuals are able to change their external bodily expressions and the associated internal dialogue. Remember that unresourceful behaviours are learnt unconsciously when we are young and without the experience and learnt intelligence to do something different that we have as adults.

A note about limiting beliefs

Habits in thinking can result in the formation of beliefs. Beliefs are developed to make sense of the world and are formed from significant emotional events and the environment in the fullest sense, including peers, schooling, role models and the unconscious modelling of parents and others, as part of a much bigger list. Bavister and Vickers (2004: 68) suggest that beliefs are 'not fixed' although often treated as fact. Wake (2010: 156) describes them as 'convictions' held 'to be true'.

They can be positive, however; they can also be restrictive and self-fulfilling. Strongly held beliefs can prevent individuals from registering information which contradicts the belief. This then becomes limiting. Bavister and Vickers (2004: 69) report that Dilts and DeLozier identified three specific ways individuals 'limit themselves':

- **hopelessness** – when individuals choose to believe it is not possible to achieve something, or that there is no hope;
- **helplessness** – when individuals believe something is possible, but do not think they are capable of it;
- **worthlessness** – when individuals do not believe they deserve to attain something.

Dilts and DeLozier suggest that these limiting beliefs are difficult for individuals to recognise and change.

ACTIVITY 3.1

Thoughts and behaviour

This activity requires two people. One person is asked to think of a behaviour that he or she wants to change, for example repeated late arrival at meetings. With curiosity, the second person asks the following questions, while taking note of the breathing, expression, tone and demeanour of the person providing the answers:

- *What exactly are you thinking at the moment you are late?*
- *How do you see yourself?*
- *How are you behaving?*
- *What are you feeling?*
- *What are you saying to yourself?*

TIPS FOR SUCCESS

- *Be aware of what you tell yourself and how you feel in any given moment; this will enable you, as a manager, to create greater flexibility through understanding how different situations, people and your own internal dialogue have an impact on behaviour. This increased awareness will generate opportunities and choices to change the thoughts, internal dialogue and resultant feeling in yourself and others.*
- *Having a greater appreciation of how people behave and react will improve your ability to match their responses more appropriately.*
- *With an increased awareness you will realise that there is a choice in how an individual can react to a set of circumstances. This is very empowering.*

Section 4
Creating positive mind solutions

Thinking differently is an important theme in this section, which discusses the impact of habitual negative thinking and the effect on the body.

Creating positive mind solutions is the process of deliberately generating positive or helpful mind solutions or 'good brain juice' and is based on the fact that the mind and body are integrally linked. An individual's thoughts create a soup of chemicals which directly affect every part of the body. Neill (2009: 99) cites John La Valle, an executive supercoach, as using the phrase 'good brain juice'.

Chemical messengers (brain juice)

Behaviour is the consequence of millions of brain cells, or neurons, communicating with each other via chemical and electrical processes using neurotransmitters, neuropeptides and hormones. The neurons are responsible for sending and receiving messages to help the brain maintain homeostasis and provide normal body functions.

There are three types of neurons: sensory neurons, which convert environmental stimuli into electrical impulses that are transmitted to the brain; motor neurons, which transmit signals from the brain to muscles, glands and other effector cells; and the interneurons, located in the central nervous system, which acts as a bridge between the sensory and motor neurones.

Neuropeptides (small, protein-like molecules) are released in the bloodstream, for example endorphin, which attaches to receptor sites particularly around the heart, chest and internal viscera (soft internal organs of the abdominal and chest cavity). The neurotransmitters produce and act on cells via electrochemical signals. Aspartic acid is an example; low levels produce a feeling of tiredness and depression. Phenylethylamine is another neurotransmitter, which increases with exercise and has an antidepressant effect. It is also found in chocolate. Figure 4.1 depicts the range of impact the neurotransmitters have on the body.

Imbalances in the neurotransmitters in terms of either too little or too much create a number of effects from anxiety and insomnia to fatigue and lack of motivation depending on the type of neurotransmitter. There are three key important neurotransmitters which affect a person's mood, which can be seen in Table 4.1.

One of the causes of neurotransmitter imbalances is high levels of stress or emotional trauma (McEwen, 2000; Kloet, Joels and Holsboer, 2005; Arnsten, 2009; Roozendaal, McEwen and Chattarji, 2009). This can be further compounded by an individual's sensitivity to stress (Kaufman *et al.*, 2000; Kloet, Joels and Holsboer, 2005).

If every thought produces a chemical effect within the brain and a resultant signal to the body, the impact of continued stressful, angry and negative self-limiting thoughts can, over

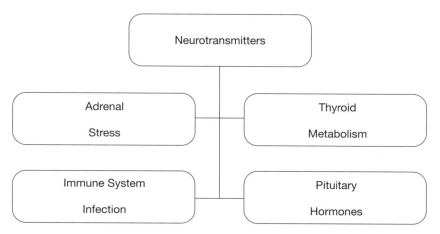

Figure 4.1 The important role neurotransmitters play in regulating the body

Table 4.1 Neurotransmitters which affect a person's mood

	Low levels of this neurotransmitter produce:
Serotonin	Restlessness, difficulty sleeping, low mood.
Noradrenaline	Impacts on the body's ability to set and regulate energy levels, and impacts on mental focus and motivation.
Dopamine	Loss of pleasure and satisfaction.

time, be potentially damaging. Anger, for example, increases the heart rate and blood pressure. The process of a thought, which creates a feeling, which then produces further thoughts and feelings is described by Dispenza (2007: 43) as a 'continuous cycle'. He uses the example of someone who is insecure continually thinking that he or she is 'not good enough', and describes how the brain in response produces chemicals to match the insecure feeling, resulting in the person feeling the way he or she is thinking; this feeling in turn produces insecure thoughts, and the cycle continues.

Through personal awareness, or consciousness, individuals can become attuned to what chemical messages or 'brain juice' they are producing. This can be 'good brain juice' or 'bad brain juice'. The easiest way to realise the type of 'brain juice' is to ask: What am I feeling right now? Am I feeling comfortable or uncomfortable?

An individual's unconscious does not have the ability to judge and therefore the capability to differentiate between what is good and what is bad. Good and bad therefore don't really exist, as they are subjective judgements that are created, based on a person's upbringing, values and beliefs. The brain cannot discern the difference between invented or imaginary dreams and reality; you may be fantasising about the worst scenarios of an event in the comfort and safety of your home, but the brain produces the equivalent stress neurochemicals, which in the long term can cause harm and physical damage. It is, therefore, contingent on what attachments and significance we give to events in our lives.

Depending on the meaning we create, the mind will produce the relevant 'brain juice'. This allows the body to react in accordance with the thoughts generated (Dispenza, 2007).

Table 4.2 Examples of good and bad brain juice

Good brain juice	Bad brain juice
Love	Rejection
Success	Anger
Freedom	Frustration
Intimacy	Loneliness
Security	Depression
Adventure	Failure
Power	Humiliation
Passion	Guilt
Comfort	Boredom
Health	Inadequacy
Pride	Stress
Contribution	Anxiety

Source: Holroyd and Ross (2011: 23)

Dispenza (2007) suggests that, when people are in a state of distress, anxiety or depression, or at a point of a major life transition, they are more prone to illness. The immune system and, in particular, the white blood cells potentially function differently, especially as a result of prolonged stress. Dispenza (2007) has concluded that thoughts can create physical manifestations in the body. The quality of 'brain juice', or neurochemical cocktail, affects not only our ability to think clearly and be resourceful, but also how healthy we are and how healthy we stay.

An experiment was carried out at Stanford University where individuals received something decadent to eat, for example chocolate or something of their choice. Those who ate it with guilt or shame experienced transient decreases in immune function, whereas those who enjoyed the experience had a positive surge in immune status (Monti, 2000).

This knowledge is integrally linked to maintaining resourceful and important emotional states of healthy well-being. An essential aspect of 'self-management is the ability to manage own emotion and be resilient in a range of complex and demanding situations' (NHS Leadership Quality Framework, in Gray, Field and Brown, 2010: 207). To a leader of oneself or others, this key understanding of the importance of producing 'good brain juice' is essential in maintaining resilience. 'Resilience' comes from the Latin *resilire* meaning to 'leap back', the capacity to recover quickly from difficulties. Whether in the form of viewing problems as challenges and opportunities to learn and grow or changing our thoughts to see setbacks not as failure but as feedback, resilience becomes about how we think.

> *It is not the strongest of the species that survive, nor the most intelligent, but the most responsive to change.*
>
> (Charles Darwin, British naturalist, 1809–82)

Goleman (1998: 77) suggests that individuals who can adapt to shifting challenges by changing their perspective of things not only survive burn-out and stress but thrive in stressful environments. He describes experiments which showed that 'resilient' people recovered much more rapidly from stress than their less resilient counterparts. This is exemplified in the following self-reflections of two different people:

Social worker A   'I'm always chasing my tail, like a hamster in a wheel, filling in all this paperwork. I'm drowning in it, never able to catch up.'

Social worker B   'We have to complete the standard paperwork; it's part of the job. I don't let it get to me; I find the fun in all that I do.'

Communicating like social worker B is therefore important for mental health and well-being.

What the research says

- Over time, stress can produce 'structural changes' in the brain potentially causing 'depression, post-traumatic stress disorder and individual differences in the aging process' (McEwen, 2000: 172).
- However, the long-term effects of early stress in child abuse cases can be moderated by the quality of the subsequent relationships in the caregiving environment (Kaufman *et al.*, 2000).
- The pre-frontal cortex (PFC), which is the area of the brain involved in the 'highest order cognitive abilities', is the area which is most adversely affected by stress (Arnsten, 2009: 410).
- The amygdala area of the brain is involved in encoding significant emotional experiences; the effectiveness of this process is adversely affected by severe stress, which can result in a source of 'chronic anxiety' and a decrease in 'cognitive performance' (Roozendaal, McEwen and Chattarji, 2009: 423).
- Studies have demonstrated that laughter can help relieve pain and bring greater happiness and increased immunity (Bennett *et al.*, 2003).

Importantly, environmental, dietary and genetic predisposition can also have an impact in terms of the effects of stress (Kloet, Joels and Holsboer, 2005; Feder, Nestler and Charney, 2009).

ACTIVITY **4.1**

Memories that make you smile

- *Think about something that makes you immediately smile. Allow yourself to become fully immersed in this memory and relax. Carry out this activity as frequently as you are able and feel comfortable. Notice any changes this creates.*

TIPS FOR SUCCESS

- *Recognise the potentially adverse effect of stress over the long term and understand how this can be mitigated. This is beneficial in terms of resilience not only for you as a leader but for the individuals you manage.*
- *It is important to realise that changing the way an individual thinks, particularly challenging limiting beliefs and negative thinking, has real health benefits and can preserve cognitive function.*
- *Checking your feelings and, if necessary, changing your thoughts (or 'brain juice') not only create resourceful states but also have long-term benefits, especially in relation to concentration and clear thinking.*

Section 5

Representational systems and words

Individuals function within an internal world which is as profoundly unique as each human being, and the external world is filtered through 'representational systems'. Representational systems are the focus of this section.

Representational systems are the processes which are used to experience and re-present the world to ourselves. An individual takes in external information through the five senses (seeing, hearing, feeling, smelling and tasting). These five senses act like filters, filtering information from the external world and helping to convert, store and organise it and attach meaning to experiences. These same senses are used to recall information internally. Table 5.1 summarises these processes.

Experiencing the world through the five senses allows an individual to re-present and store the experience internally. These five senses are referred to as 'modalities' (Bandler, 2008b: 310) and include the following:

Visual (V)	See
Auditory (A)	Hear
Kinaesthetic (K)	Feel
Olfactory (O)	Smell
Gustatory (G)	Taste

For each of the modalities there are submodalities or sub-units which are finer characteristics. For example, visual submodalities include colour, contrast, shape, movement, brightness and size; auditory submodalities include timbre, pitch, volume, tempo, duration, and stereo or mono; and kinaesthetic submodalities include pressure, temperature, intensity, texture and location (see pages 118–121 for further information). In Western society, visual, auditory and kinaesthetic are the three dominant modalities used, and are abbreviated to VAK.

An experience is represented, coded and stored through the modalities and submodalities. Individuals can use all three primary modalities but often tend to prefer one. For example,

Table 5.1 Summary of the processes related to representational systems

Process	Representational system	Description
INTERNAL (input)	See, feel, hear, smell and taste	How we prefer to gather information.
THOUGHTS (thinking)	See, feel, hear, smell and taste	How we process information internally.
EXTERNAL (output)	See, feel, hear, smell and taste	How we express ourselves.

some people can make clear mental images and think mainly in pictures; others find this difficult and may choose to talk to themselves, or base their actions on a feel for the situation. Bandler and Grinder (1975a), when observing individuals, found that the words used indicated which representational system they preferred, and matching with the same types of words created noticeably better rapport.

The concept of a preferred representational system, for example visual, evidenced by someone using words like 'I see' and 'the focus is on', is context specific, about what is happening in the moment, which means that this can be fleeting. It is therefore a mistake to label individuals as being, for example, 'visual', as the senses change depending upon the internal and external influences. Individuals may also use more than one representation system at a time. What is different from one person to another is which sense people are using and more specifically the differences in the submodalities (discussed further in Section 11).

Table 5.2 Some words identified within each modality

Seeing words (visual):

Analyse	Examine	Image	Picture
Survey	Angle	Focus	Vision
Appear	Inspect	Foresee	Aspect
Scene	Scan	Illustrate	View
Notice	Glow	Scope	Scrutinise
Hindsight	Oversight	Obscure	Demonstrate
Horizon	Panorama	Idea	Glimpse
Obvious	Show	Portray	Brilliant
Pattern	Spotless	Hazy	Notice
Envision	Observe	Look	Show
See	Clear	Illuminate	Reveal
Eye	Bright	Shape	Envision
Perspective	Imagine	Screen	Dark
Mirror	Insight	Blind	Reflect

Hearing words (auditory):

Announce	Earshot	Mention	Noise
State	Speak	Talk	Tell
Hear	Shrill	Screech	Aloud
Silence	Sound	Report	Gossip
Loud	Listen	Roar	Tone
Pronounce	Vocal	Hush	Squeal
Utter	Proclaim	Interview	Speechless
Communicate	Discuss	Remark	Inquire
Argue	Call	Mutter	Chat
Discuss	Shout	Narrate	Groan
Dialogue	Attune	Resonate	Harmonise
Articulate	Volume	Amplify	Pitch
Alarmed	Outspoken	Babble	Verbose

Table 5.2 Continued

Feeling words (kinaesthetic):

Active flow	Hustle	Set	Hold
Intuition	Shallow	Tension	Lukewarm
Shift	Tied	Softly	Motion
Touch	Muddled	Solid	Touch
Unbearable	Panicky	Sore	Unsettled
Feel	Pressure	Stir	Impression
Firm hunch	Sensitive	Stress	Stir
Absorb	Attach	Support	Sturdy
Take	Hold	Point	Cool
Fall	Hot	Worry	Stiff

Source: Adapted from Holroyd and Ross (2011)

When interpreting an experience through the five senses this remains an individual perception and not the actual reality. We do not all think in the same way. Indeed, Bandler and Grinder (1975a) observed people's subjective experiences; they noticed that people's memories occurred in a specific sequence of the individual's representational systems, and they called these strategies.

Sensory acuity

As human beings we are predisposed to making sense of the world, looking for patterns, clues for danger or threats to our survival, and this is achieved through what we see, hear, feel, taste and smell. To understand how someone else processes the same information it is important to increase our 'sensory acuity'. Sensory acuity is described by Bradbury as 'the skill of being sensitive to a person's non-verbal changes (rate of speech, skin colour, muscle tension etc), which give clues to their mental activity' (2010: 165).

This ability to notice in the moment requires the skill of detachment from our own internal references and usual filtering processes to become aware of, and open to, someone else's. When speaking to someone, notice the words the person uses and match these to create better rapport. Matching establishes a sense of trust and understanding. This appreciation will provide essential information about whether what you are saying is being received in the way you wanted and anticipated. The following sentences contain examples of visual modalities:

Junior member of staff: 'I can see clearly how this report will have an impact.'
Manager: 'Clearly it is useful and illustrates the point well; you could consider presenting this to the group.'

During a conversation, this information may previously have gone undetected, as individuals concentrate and rehearse in their heads what they are going to say next, and perhaps become anxious in a group setting as they practise a question or statement. Learning to relax, become detached and notice can be practised and may be best applied when it is not crucial, for example in a café. Creating enough time and a 'pause' to read the information sufficiently in the moment takes practice but can be learnt. As Kouzes and Posner (2007: 204) suggest, 'the only way that people can learn is by doing things they've never done before'.

ACTIVITY **5 . 1**

Stories with visual, auditory and kinaesthetic words

This activity involves groups of four or more:

- **Person A** *starts a story with one sentence, using visual representational words.*
- **Person B** *continues with a second sentence, using auditory words.*
- **Person C** *continues with a third sentence, using kinaesthetic words.*
- **Person D** *continues with a fourth sentence, using visual words.*

While completing the exercise, note which representational system you find the easiest and which the most difficult.

In meetings, it is useful to notice what went well and what did not, remembering what was said, how that made you feel and what you observed about other people's reactions. Reflecting in this way will also increase your sensory acuity.

ACTIVITY **5 . 2**

Combining the representational systems

This activity involves groups of four or more:

- **Person A** *starts a story with one sentence, using representational words that are visual.*
- **Person B** *continues with a second sentence, using first visual words (from the last person) and then auditory words.*
- **Person C** *continues with a third sentence, using the auditory words (from the last person) and then kinaesthetic words.*
- **Person D** *continues with a fourth sentence, using first kinaesthetic words (from the last person) and then visual words.*

Continue one sentence at a time, changing the representational system each time after first using the previous person's statement.

Again notice which representational system you find the easiest and which the most difficult.

For example:

- A: *'I walked into the office and I saw my boss with a client.'*
- B: *'I saw them talking and I could hear the tone of their voice.'*
- C: *'The conversation sounded tense and that made me feel concerned.'*
- D: *'The client was upset and I could see that my boss was trying to comfort her.'*
- E: *'It was clear how she felt, and the sound of her voice was sad.'*

TIPS FOR SUCCESS

- *To improve communication it is important for you as a leader to identify in the moment an individual's preferences, thereby maximising the effectiveness of the interaction and gaining and maintaining rapport.*
- *In written communication or in delivering presentations it is important that you cover all the representational systems to improve the success of conveying the right message.*
- *This is particularly important in change management. Teams especially perform better when there is good communication, which in turn creates trusting relationships, an important component of effective change management (Blanchard, 2007).*
- *Wake (2010: 54) suggests matching email communication to people with a visual preference, matching focus groups or telephone calls to auditory-sensitive people, and having one-to-one meetings with kinaesthetic people.*

Section 6
Anchoring

The way an individual represents the world can be further hardwired by something called 'anchoring' (O'Connor, 2001: 76). This section discusses anchoring in detail.

According to Hayes, anchoring is 'a way of gaining access to, and being able to hold on to, the states we need in order to be successful in a given context' (2006: 69). Anchoring is a process that is also known as a conditional reflex. This was made popular in the West through the writings of John B. Watson (1913) and related to the idea of conditioning as an automatic form of learning. It was a concept identified by the Russian psychologist Ivan Pavlov, who was awarded a Nobel Prize for his work in 1904. Pavlov's research greatly influenced science as well as popular culture, and the phrase 'Pavlov's dog' is often used to describe someone who reacts to an event rather than uses critical thinking (Churches and Terry, 2010: 106).

Walker (2004) suggests that, while classical conditioning is concerned with an external stimulus, NLP would include internal thoughts and responses too. O'Connor (2001: 76) states that 'anchors are all around us', spontaneously evident in everyday experiences which can change an individual's mood from one moment to the next. From the time we are born we learn to classify information, experiences and events, and attach meaning. These values and interpretations are anchored to the experiences, which become uniquely subjective for each individual.

We have all, therefore, experienced anchoring on some level, as it is a natural phenomenon. We hear a song and it reminds us of something we experienced in the past. We see something and feel a certain way. An anchor is, in essence, any presentation (internally or externally generated) which triggers a memory that we access through another one of the senses. An internal emotional state is subsequently produced to match the remembered one (Churches and Terry, 2010). In anchoring, we adapt an aspect or small part of an experience to elicit and recreate the whole experience (Hall, 2007). For example, the smell of a perfume can instantly take an individual back to a specific occasion. This is a normal occurrence; in order to give meaning to things our minds will automatically connect experiences (O'Connor and Seymour, 2002).

Most of us have encountered positive anchoring when communicating and reaching a certain level of rapport and understanding. Maybe at times, however, the flow of conversation or discussion changed, the interaction became more tense, strained or difficult, and you wished that you had a way of re-accessing those positive experiences. Anchoring is a process which allows an individual to re-access positive experiences repeatedly. Hall would suggest that 'Anchoring provides a way to handle experiences or manage internal subjective experiences such as memories, emotional states, and so on, so as to sequence them in new ways or frame them for more resourcefulness' (2007: 61).

Anchors are like a bridge that connects a present event to an emotion created by a similar occurrence in the past. Skilled leaders, with this knowledge, will have an understanding of and be able to access more resourceful and positive anchors or states, for example when they need to be confident, highly motivated and creative. This is particularly important in developing and maintaining communication with people about difficult and complex matters, issues and ideas.

O'Connor (2001) describes this type of anchoring as 'resource anchoring', where an anchor is deliberately set in order to change an emotional state to bring positive resources into the situation, and suggests these are useful when:

- taking a test;
- giving a presentation;
- having a difficult meeting;
- dealing with stressful situations;
- engaging in public speaking;
- making a difficult decision.

Negative states, however, can also be anchored with associations or triggers which generate bad feelings and more unresourceful states. Hall (2007), for instance, talks about individuals having dozens or hundreds of ways in which to 'feel bad'.

An event from childhood, for example, may have anchored a negative emotion towards talking in front of an audience. In the present time, public speaking may feel uncomfortable and overwhelming. If leaders have this appreciation and understanding of anchoring, it will allow them to recognise the negative anchors, which can then be broken or collapsed (O'Connor, 2001).

Important points to remember about anchoring

- Anchors do not need to be conditioned over long periods. An anchor can be created rapidly, for the brain can quickly make associations and connections.
- Repeated stimuli can reinforce an anchor (stacking anchors).
- Anchors can be assimilated after one interaction or exposure, for example in the formation of phobias.
- Internal experience (i.e. cognitive behaviour) is considered to be as significant behaviourally as a behaviour that can be seen and measured.
- The more intense the emotional experience which an individual has at the time that the anchor is 'set' (when the trigger stimulus is applied), the stronger the response will be when the anchor is 'fired off' (re-introduced) at a later time. A trigger can be created by pressing the index finger against the thumb at the peak of the experience.
- In creating an anchor, the timing of the trigger stimulus is critical if it is to be associated with the desired state (Hall, 2007; Churches and Terry, 2010).

Figure 6.1 illustrates the ideal timing which corresponds to the final increase and peaking of the intensity of the state, which is then anchored at this point (Molden, 2007).

- The more unique the stimulus, the more accurate it will be in re-accessing the desired state.
- The more accurately the stimulus is replicated, the more quickly the original associated stimulus can be re-accessed.
- Anchors can be established in all the senses, for example external or internal sights, sounds, feelings, smells and tastes.

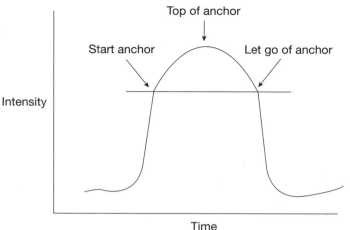

Figure 6.1
Installation of an anchor

- Anchors can be used in an obvious or less obvious way, depending on the outcome. Most of the time anchors are made openly and unconsciously.
- For many people, a single word can create a very strong positive or negative response (O'Connor, 2001).

What the research says

- In a control trial Brandis (1987) was able to show some changes in using anchors with parents who demonstrated anger towards their children.
- Squirrel (2009) used a number of techniques including anchoring with a small group of children who demonstrated degrees of social, emotional and behavioural difficulties, and found that in almost all aspects of learning and behaviour the group had improved more than the control group.

In summary, according to O'Connor and Seymour, 'Using your resourceful states through anchors is one of the most effective ways to change your own and other people's behaviour' (2002: 55). In the process the 'well-being' of an individual and/or team is focused on, maintained and promoted.

Blanchard (2007) discusses the importance of 'flexibility' in leadership, particularly when managing change and others, and describes this as an important and integral ingredient in creating sustainable change. Being able to manage emotional states creates this flexibility.

TIPS FOR SUCCESS

- *Try to recollect times or situations when an individual was confident or motivated and anchor the state to now. This ability to reproduce a productive state is very beneficial in any capacity.*
- *Using specific 'anchoring' to elicit states of confidence and enthusiasm in presentations, meetings and discussions is a useful approach when you are leading others.*
- *Help individuals to anchor more resourceful states; this is extremely valuable to you as a manager.*

Part 2

Becoming an exquisite communicator

Section 7
Understanding communication

How is it that we are able to communicate? How do we understand the words that we have learnt? How do we know to arrange the words in the right order? Is there a better way to communicate to ensure understanding is clear? And how can we positively influence others?

Argyle (1994) would describe two important elements of communication in the form of a conversation as non-verbal and verbal. Throughout a conversation the speaker and listener will demonstrate 'continuous facial expressions', gestures and other non-verbal actions. Verbal speech conveys information, has a grammatical format and has sentences which principally express meaning (Argyle, 1994: 23).

The aim of learning and understanding how communication works is so that we can improve the way we communicate with others. In the workplace, communication is driven by the need for information about the people in that environment, irrespective of which type of communication is required. There is a skill to communicating so that we are able to send and receive information effectively. Successful communicators have the ability to overcome the barriers of communication through understanding the content and the feelings that others are trying to communicate.

These tools and techniques began with the study of excellent communicators: Virginia Satir, a family therapist; Fritz Perls, the founder of Gestalt therapy; and Milton Erickson, a medical hypnotherapist (Hall, 2001). These individuals were modelled and, as part of this process, the specific skills and competencies they exhibited were identified. These included the crucial elements of rapport and non-verbal communication.

In this section, the importance of rapport building and non-verbal communication for leaders will be explored further. To communicate more effectively it is essential to cultivate the capacity to create rapport (Hall, 2007; Churches and Terry, 2010).

Rapport

Rapport is the ability to relate to others in a way that creates a climate of trust and understanding. The purpose of rapport is to establish a feeling of comfort and commonality between people using non-verbal communication (body language) to ensure that an individual feels more relaxed in conversations or meetings; essentially it is subconscious communication (O'Connor and Seymour, 2002).

> *Rapport is the ability to enter someone else's world, to make him feel that you understand him, that you have a strong common bond. It's the ability to go fully from your map of the world to his map of the world. It's the essence of successful communication.*
>
> (Robbins, 1987: 260)

Goleman (2002: 51) would suggest that skilled leaders manage good relationships by 'building rapport'. In doing so, they not only influence individuals but also build trust; in the process of establishing rapport the individual is also 'consensus building', which is described by Goleman (1998: 171) as essential in gaining the support of others in leading change through people. Building rapport can be as simple as sharing a story about oneself which closely matches the listener's experience. When individuals offer additional information other than what is requested (especially personal information), rapport is clearly evident.

Non-verbal communication

There are, however, two aspects to communication: Argyle *et al.* (1970) proposed the hypothesis that, whereas spoken language is normally used for communicating information about events external to the speakers, non-verbal codes are used to establish and maintain interpersonal relationships.

Navarro (2008) describes non-verbal communication as a means of conveying information just like speech, except that it is attained through facial expressions, touch (haptic communication), gestures, body language or posture, physical movements, body adornments such as clothes or jewellery, and the non-verbal elements of speech, for example voice quality, emotion, tone and timbre.

Non-verbal communication has been reported to account for 60–65 per cent of communication (Navarro, 2008: 4). Mehrabian has been quoted as stating that the spoken word is a mere 7 per cent, while tone is 38 per cent and body language 55 per cent, totalling the non-verbal part of our communication at 93 per cent (Borg, 2008: 17). However, this representation is accurate only in circumstances where one is expressing feelings or attitude; the context was artificial, and his study included only women. Furthermore, Hall (1984) would suggest that women are better at non-verbal communication than men.

Nevertheless, non-verbal communication is still a larger part of our communication process, and Navarro (2008) reports that those who can effectively interpret and understand non-verbal communication will be more successful. It is a mistake, however, to interpret only the non-verbal gesture of the whole conversation. People with their hands folded in front of them are not necessarily closed to ideas but possibly cold or simply comfortable. There are some gestures that are universal (Ekman, 2003). When people are happy, they smile, while nodding of the head is almost common to all to show affirmation, a 'yes' signal.

In order to understand non-verbal communication we have to pay attention to the big picture: what speakers are doing with their bodies as well as to the properties of the voice. One can get as detailed as observing a person's facial expression and dilation of the eyes, which is a result of one or more motions of the facial muscles. The movements made convey different emotions that are being experienced at that moment and are almost involuntary and mostly unconscious.

The biggest advantage of learning and understanding body language is to learn more about the self and how to improve relationships with others (Goleman, 1998; Ekman, 2003). This links importantly to creating greater self-awareness and better open communication, or of being more able, as Blanchard (2007: 72) advises, to 'partner for performance' in a new leadership paradigm of facilitating change through empowerment.

In addition, understanding body language facilitates the ability to be more effective by making sure that the non-verbal communication signals are congruent (in sync) with the spoken words. For example, in meetings you may start to notice when the speaker says something like 'We totally believe in this system and will do our best to support it' and at the same time is moving his or her head from left to right, giving a negative, 'no', non-verbal signal.

Typically, when people are happy you will see it in their eyes; they smile, and their bodies will be relaxed. People may be asked how they are today; an automatic response of 'Fine' is given, yet all their non-verbal signals suggest they are not. Learning to be congruent helps individuals to appear trustworthy and to be more effective, and utilising non-verbal communication purposefully to match and support verbal responses will improve the individuals' impact (O'Connor and Seymour, 2002).

Building rapport

Leadership is a relationship.

(Kouzes and Posner, 2007: 24)

Building rapport is an important part of communication and one of the most productive activities (Molden, 2007). Given that non-verbal communication forms the main part of communication, it goes without saying that a good communicator would pay attention not only to what is being said, but to what is not being said.

The reason that rapport building is so effective is that the unconscious will notice what is different and likes what is similar. By removing the differences between the individual and the speaker and by matching or mirroring movements, you will build more similarities, which creates an environment of likeness. We naturally feel a kinship with people who have a similar background to us, and that is why, in life in general, people will find individuals with the same cultural background to form a community. Rapport is also associated with the capability to see each other's point of view, to be on the same wavelength and to appreciate the feelings of others. The aim is to be able to establish rapport with any person, at any moment in time. O'Connor (2001: 39) states that 'to be influential in any relationship we need rapport'. When people are like each other, they 'like each other' (Molden, 2007: 157). Rapport, however, is a process of responsiveness, not necessarily simply 'liking' someone.

Good communicators who know the secrets to this mysterious language use it to get results. They learn to observe, interpret and communicate on all the verbal and non-verbal levels. They are able to utilise more than just words to convey their ideas and influence the opinion of others.

Being able to use this in a situation of conflict will help to turn things around. Rapport can be established quickly by building trust through matching the voice tempo, breathing rate and rate of speech, and once rapport has been established the tone can be slowly brought down to a calmer one, creating a more amicable environment where conflict can be resolved. You know that rapport has been established if the other person follows. The person you are communicating with will feel understood and listened to.

It is the non-verbal communication that people see, hear or feel consciously or unconsciously that helps them to know how they feel about someone. When an individual walks into the room and feels confident and relaxed, we instinctively know it. What we are actually doing is reading their non-verbal signals. Thoughts, for example, create micro facial expressions which are automatic and involuntary. How you feel about yourself and what type of person you are relate to your posture and the energy radiating from you. That is what people instinctively read.

Indeed, McMaster and Grinder (1993: xiv) would suggest that non-verbal communication is the 'most influential' and 'most dominant' of the two forms of communication.

Individuals also prefer to speak to someone who uses words that match their own representational system (for example seeing, hearing, feeling or internal dialogue), a point made earlier, which is worth repeating, by a ratio of three to one (Brockman, 1981). Below are some examples which are introduced here and further expanded upon in Section 11:

Seeing

Language used: Look, see, imagine, appear, blind, focus, view, bright, glow, neat, observe, picture, reveal, stare, sunny, vision, examine, glance, brilliant.

Phrases used: Look at this, see it, watch this, show me, dark side, in light of, glowing review, look into, see what you mean, the picture's clear, let's focus on, that's your clear view/perspective.

Hearing

Language used: Hear, say, chat, talk, call, announce, discuss, speak, lecture, listen, noisy, quiet, ring, questions, silence, tell, told, tune, voice, grumble.

Phrases used: Sounds good, I hear you, let's talk about it, call me, ask them/me, it sounds right, argue the point, you voiced it well, hear me out, let's discuss this further, that could strike a chord, ring me and we can talk some more.

Feeling

Language used: Feel, absorb, attack, balance, cutting, fall, fear, flat, hurt, hard, each, touch, tender, steady, shake up, worry, impression, contact, grasp.

Phrases used: Get a feel for, too hot to handle, make it tangible, go for it, solid base, tough to deal with, get a grip on things, make an impression, contact me again, you've grasped it, you're in control.

Also see the examples in Section 5.

The use of the right words is important in the communication exchange. However, as discussed earlier, non-verbal components of communication are also vital. These are now examined in more detail.

Advanced non-verbal communication

Gestures

While people are talking they constantly move their hands, body and head to correspond with their speech. Argyle (1994: 34) describes this as part of 'total communication'. Individuals may also point to the sense organ they are using internally; for example, when listening to sounds in their head they may be touching or pointing to their ears (O'Connor and Seymour, 2002).

Replicating someone's facial gestures subtly shows that you accept the person. Laughing at people's jokes, or using signs of approval while they are speaking, sends an unconscious message that you agree with what they are saying. It is important to remember that any false gestures will be detected. The importance of having a positive regard throughout is essential.

Facial expressions and blinking

One of the main purposes of facial expressions, besides providing an instant commentary on a conversation, is to convey 'emotional states' and a standpoint such as 'hostility' or 'liking' (Argyle, 1994: 25).

Ekman (2003) identified universal facial expressions recognised around the world, which are the same for all cultures:

- happiness;
- fear;
- surprise;
- sadness;
- anger;
- disgust; and
- contempt.

Importantly, these facial expressions cannot be disguised. The format and presentation are distinct and universal.

Ekman (2003: 130) suggests that, if muscular movements for an emotion are expressed facially, 'that emotion will generally begin to occur'. This is the same for smiling, which is the universal sign for enjoyment. Ekman (2003: 191) advises that there are many 'enjoyable emotions': contentment, excitement, wonderment, amusement, relief, ecstasy and gratitude are some examples. How do we distinguish them? Ekman (2003) advocates that it is the voice that denotes the distinction.

Anger signals pending problems and is evidenced in both facial expressions and vocal responses (Ekman, 2003). Women and men do not differ in their rates of spontaneous blinking (Doughty, 2002). When we feel angry or negative towards something, our pupils contract. Our blinking rate increases when we feel under pressure, for example when constructing (lying).

Churches and Terry (2010) report that Richard Bandler and John Grinder discovered that eye movements can reveal what the brain is focusing on, by displaying if we are imagining or remembering something, and they suggested that, when the eyes look up, this implies some involvement of the visual internal representation, and accessing. When the eyes look to the side, auditory processing is occurring. When they look down, feelings or emotions are being accessed. Typically, 35 per cent of people prefer to remember something visually, and may say 'I see what you mean'; 25 per cent will use the auditory aspect, and could say 'That sounds familiar'; and the remaining 40 per cent use the feeling preference, perhaps saying 'We reached an understanding' (O'Connor and Lages, 2004; Churches and Terry, 2010).

Mouth

Smiling is a universal and complimenting gesture (Ekman, 2003). This shows that you like and trust someone, which will then reflect safety for the person to like and trust you (Ekman and Friesen, 2003).

Smiles can be difficult to read, for people will smile as a greeting or to hide other expressions such as fear, anger, disgust or sadness. However, a real smile as opposed to a false smile involves the muscles around the eyes (the orbicularis oculi). These muscles, according to Ekman (2003), cannot be voluntarily contracted. In essence, they are the muscles that make the eyes smile.

With a false smile, you will see that the lips remain closed, the mouth is drawn straight back, and there is little engagement with the eyes. The face generally looks tense. In a true smile, the eyes are engaged, the corners of the mouth are drawn up towards the cheekbones, and the mouth is open, revealing teeth. The face is relaxed (Ekman, 2003).

A closed mouth is also a sign of distress. You will see that the lip muscles tighten. When emotions are extreme the lips disappear and the corners of the mouth turn down.

Watch out for pursed lips; they are a sign that someone is not in agreement, or that the person's thinking differs from yours (Navarro, 2008). When someone is nervous, you will see nail biting, lip licking, chewing of the lips and lip plucking – these are all self-pacifying functions which release calming chemicals (Ekman, 2003).

Sneers are signs of disrespect. Observe for these particularly when a suggestion or idea is expressed.

Nose

Crinkling the nose upwards is a sign of disgust (Ekman, 2003). This gesture is used when we don't like something in the extreme (Navarro, 2008). In a conversation this gesture will be very subtle and quick, with the message 'I don't like what I hear' or 'Something stinks.'

Actual nose flaring signals that someone is about to do something physical, like climb the stairs, while nasal wing dilation can be a sign that an individual is going to attack and is, therefore, dangerous (Navarro, 2008).

Eyes

When we put our hands over our eyes as if to block the view, this usually means that we don't like what we have just heard. Touching the eyes during a conversation may mean that people feel uncomfortable and needs to calm themselves. Closing one's eyes is another unconscious way to block negative emotions (Navarro, 2008). Frowning is an unconscious signal of distress, anger or confusion (Ekman, 2003). Certain brow and forehead positions are used to exaggerate a particular word or comment, like using punctuation in written language (Ekman and Friesen, 2003).

Neck

Touching the back of the neck is a sign of discomfort, insecurity and doubt and in some cases even fear (Navarro, 2008). This gesture may follow touching the front of the neck, or adjusting one's tie or necklace, and, for women in particular, touching the hollow area between the Adam's apple and breastbone (the 'neck dimple') is done in order to pacify themselves when in a distressed state or when they feel threatened, uncomfortable, insecure or fearful (Navarro, 2008). Men prefer to stroke or touch their faces; these actions are to help calm rather than solve problems (Navarro, 2008).

Breathing

Breathing will indicate the rate at which we speak. So, when you observe and match the rate of someone's breathing, you will be speaking at the same rate that the person is, which is an important aspect of creating rapport (Churches and Terry, 2010). People, like animals, will puff up their chests when they want to determine territorial dominance (Navarro, 2008). When individuals are stressed, their chest movements will be more rapid as they attempt to take in more oxygen as a natural response to prepare for fight or flight (Navarro, 2008).

Voice and tempo

Linked to breathing is the pace of your voice, and matching it to the normal rhythm of breathing will create attention in the listener. Pauses created in natural speech, although hardly noticeable, create a sense of anticipation and, therefore, an individual is more likely to concentrate on what is said.

The voice tone is also a crucial part of communicating. Figure 7.1 depicts some of the different voice tones and the impact.

When influencing, the command tone is most effective. Ending a suggestion with a descending tone will increase the gravitas and impact.

Voice projection is also important, particularly when presenting. This is the vocal ability to speak both loudly and clearly, using the abdominal muscles to breathe and assist in ensuring the sound is audible even over distances.

Summary

Table 7.1 is a summary of the body language and representational systems; they are generalisations and so only a guide (O'Connor and Lages, 2004: 184). People are individuals who cannot easily be delineated into groups.

Further practice for increasing sensory acuity

Practice can be achieved in daily conversations. It is important to remain out of your own head and instead direct your full attention to the individual(s) in front of you. Distracting self-talk can be minimised by:

• taking a deep breath in through your mouth, exhaling through your nose and visualising your thoughts travelling down out of your head to the ground and dissolving;
• placing the tip of your tongue behind your front teeth and relaxing your jaw. This movement distracts and gets you out of your head.

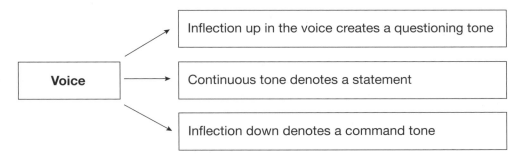

Figure 7.1 The impact of different voice tones

Table 7.1 Body language and representational systems

	Visual	Auditory	Kinaesthetic
Eye accessing	Unfocused or up to the right or left.	In the midline.	Below the midline, usually to the right.
Voice tone and tempo	Generally rapid speech, high clear voice tone.	Melodious tone, resonant, at a medium pace, often with an underlying rhythm.	Low and deeper tonality, often low and soft, with many pauses.
Breathing	High shallow breathing in the top part of the chest.	Even breathing in the middle part of the chest.	Deeper breathing from the abdomen.
Posture and gestures	More tension in the body, with the neck extended. Often thinner (ectomorphic) body type.	Often medium (mesomorphic) body type. There may be rhythmic movements of the body as if listening to music.	Rounded shoulders, head down, relaxed muscle tone, may gesture to abdomen and midline.

TIPS FOR SUCCESS

- *Your ability to communicate well by understanding the whole conversation of verbal and non-verbal signals will not only reduce miscommunication but create enhanced relationships based on real meaning (Argyle, 1994; O'Connor and Seymour, 2002; Ekman and Friesen, 2003).*
- *The importance of understanding your own non-verbal presentations is also key in delivering the right messages and, importantly, matching what words you choose with the body language you are using to gain trust and confidence in what is being said (Ekman, 2003). In addition, remember that non-verbal self-presentation – badges like clothes, hair, voice and general style – can have a far greater impact than any words used (Argyle, 1994).*
- *Communicating effectively non-verbally and verbally is integral to managing yourself and leading others, particularly in changing and developing services (Goleman, 1998). Often the biggest complaint in any organisation is the lack of good communication. Covey (1992: 272) would suggest that one habit of highly effective, principle-centred leadership is 'to first understand before being understood – the principle of empathetic communication'.*
- *In order for you to lead change, develop effective networks, provide direction, improve organisational performance, promote equality of opportunity and diversity, encourage innovation, develop productive working relationships, provide learning opportunities for colleagues, manage a project and business processes, resolve customer service problems and develop a customer-focused approach, it is imperative that you develop good communication skills, both verbal and non-verbal.*

Section 8

Advanced questioning skills model

Another important aspect of communicating is understanding exactly what is meant and asking the right questions (O'Connor, 2001). This section focuses on advanced questioning skills.

The power of words to have an impact on our thinking and how we communicate thoughts and feelings in the language patterns we use arguably creates opportunities to enrich the interpretation and, with it, our interaction with the world. The way we represent the world to 'self' and, in turn, represent 'our world' to others is based on a reductionist process. The scope for misrepresentation and misunderstandings is great. The main theme within Sections 8, 9 and 10 is language patterns and a deeper appreciation of how to enhance these to improve how we communicate.

The advanced questioning skills model is based on the theories developed by Noam Chomsky's (1957) and Alfred Korzybski's (1933, 1948, 1994) work, which greatly influenced the tools in NLP. The model is better known as the meta-model (Hall, 2007). This is an adaptation from these works to make it useful for a service-oriented setting. There are a number of language patterns referred to in this section and in Sections 9 and 10, and in Appendix 3 there is a table of the different parts of speech to act as an aide-memoire if required.

O'Connor (2001: 138) describes questioning as extremely effective, stating that 'it is impossible not to respond to a question'. He suggests that questions can:

- extract information;
- produce information;
- give and take away choices;
- direct attention and create reality;
- challenge assumptions;
- define outcomes;
- identify strategies;
- build (or break) rapport;
- summarise;
- elicit values;
- model strategies;
- associate and dissociate.

    Examples of questions include:

- What is the most useful question I can ask right now?
- What don't I know that would make a difference if I did?

- What question would get me closer to my outcome?
- Do I need to ask a question at all?

(O'Connor, 2001: 139)

Deep and surface structure

In every conversation there is the information that we hear and then there is information that we don't. Churches and Terry (2010) report that Chomsky (1957) developed the concept that each sentence has two levels, known as 'deep structure' and 'surface structure'. Deep structure is well hidden within and is formulated by the details that we have stored from an original event or experience. Surface structure is the information that we selectively verbalise and is what people can hear us say. It is selective because there is an unconscious decision about what is going to be said and what is not.

If someone went on a seven-day holiday, it would require seven days to impart the information about the entire event accurately. Clearly, this would be an inefficient way to communicate. The facts are altered, information perceived as being less important is omitted, and finally the details are generalised to reduce the length. The listener hears a version of the truth that has been altered. For every person, the truth of an event lies in the deep structure.

The advanced questioning skills equip individuals with a different and powerful communication tool. It enables people to hear more effectively and, with an attitude of curiosity, interest and respect, they can notice what information is omitted, altered and generalised so they are able to retrieve what is relevant to the situation at hand. They can listen to and identify the surface structure, which is what actually is being said in the moment. Questioning skills are used to help uncover the deep structure of an experience to enrich the understanding.

Arguably, one of the only ways that an individual has control of a conversation is to use smart questions. This is particularly true in conflict situations, providing there is an attitude of respect and a real intention and sense of curiosity to find out more information to see how exactly the individual can be helped, and remembering the importance of tonality and the accompanying non-verbal body language to maintain rapport throughout.

Hall (2001) suggests that questioning in this way allows the managers to accomplish several purposes:

- to gather the highest-quality information;
- to respond to the language cues by asking for explicit and precise information;
- to determine the level and quality of information needed in a given context;
- to use various frames for managing the process of moving from the 'present' to the 'desired' state (see Section 13) required for goal setting.

Mismatches can commonly occur between the deep and surface structures or, quite simply, there is a loss of meaning in the translation process between the two. This can create misunderstandings.

A good leader arguably helps individuals to achieve their outcomes by using clear language. Working in teams and with people is also about reducing miscommunication to a minimum and, as much as possible, understanding the original information to ensure that there are no distortions, deletions or exaggerations, referred to as 'generalisations' (Churches and Terry, 2010).

Rose Charvet (1997) would suggest that in the above process of interpretation of the deep and surface structure the outcome is invariably creating 'our version of the world'; this is often called the 'map' (Dilts, 1999; O'Connor and Seymour, 2002; Hall, 2007).

The maps that we create

This famous reference to 'the map' and more explicitly 'the map is not the territory' by Korzybski (1933) is quoted by many authors, for example Jacobson (1996), Hall (2007) and Bandler (2008b). Its translation refers to the difference of an object that is tangible and the way individuals represent that object in their minds. Korzybski suggested that people experience the world indirectly and through their constructs. What is represented is subjective, and the way individuals react to the specific information is also determined by their personal values and beliefs.

What people think they have experienced is often missing fragments of information from the real event and is therefore similar but not the same. The biggest challenge for individuals is to be aware that the territory (which is what they see, hear and feel) is not the same as the map (which they have created and is made up from thoughts).

For instance, if there was an exact, full-scale representation of London on a map, how big would that map be? The same size as London? This is both impractical and impossible. So, in order to have a map that is useful, it has to be altered to fit. It will not be exactly the same as London but close enough to what it looks like – invariably, a representation.

Let's imagine that map. There will be symbols, for example a cross, known to represent a church. The question is: what kind of church? This lack of specific detail has been called a generalisation. Another example is a park; a green space shows the area of the park on the map, but the type of park is not specified. There are numerous other illustrations of this, such as schools, supermarkets and shopping centres.

When imagining this 'map', the small details are missed. They are left out or deleted, so that the map will fit the 'paper'. We decide what is important, focus our attention on that and leave the rest out. This process of reducing the true experience by generalising, altering and omitting information affects the reality or the true picture (Hall, 2007).

In terms of science, George Armitage Miller, an American psychologist, published his paper 'The magical number seven, plus or minus two: Some limits on our capacity for processing information' (1956) in the *Psychological Review*. He suggested that we can take in only a very small amount of information consciously but that we notice and respond to much more unconsciously. He reported that our conscious, working memory, the current immediate recall, or short-term memory, is limited to processing seven plus or minus two pieces of unrelated chunks of data, for example digits, letters, words or units. Specifically, individuals could quickly identify around seven dots without counting them. Cowan (2001) later proposed four chunks as the capacity of a young adult.

Richmond (2008) confirms that our short-term memory recall is limited to the magic number seven, although random letters are harder to remember than numbers. She does suggest that using mnemonics and associations in the long-term memory can improve the recall of digits; however, the short-term recall, or ability to hold distinct pieces of information, remains at seven.

Our unconscious, by contrast, is all that we have learnt: our past experiences and all that we might notice but do not. Something is unconscious, for example, when it is not in the present moment of awareness. The background sounds that you can hear were probably unconscious to you until they were mentioned.

Most people are unaware of this process and so live as if what is in their memory is exactly true and real (O'Connor and Seymour, 2002). As we begin to realise how we are able to change an event or an experience through our individual and 'unique filtering process', we gain personal power to make changes. An understanding and a realisation of this empower an individual to question feelings and events rather than take them for granted.

In much the same way as the above, individuals, through life experiences, create maps which they automatically and unconsciously follow. The question to ask is: 'Does your map of the world work for you?' Do we have a map that will take us to where we want to go? Does it allow us to feel resourceful? Usually, our limitation is that we are unaware that the lack of resources we feel resides within our map (Covey, 1992).

EXAMPLE

If our map says 'Flying is too scary' and we need to fly, it would not be a very useful map. If our map does not take us to where we want to go, we need to change it. If we aren't getting where we want to go, then we need to stop and ask for directions from someone who knows. Therefore, as individuals pay attention to their unique internal maps, this means that there are many different maps; indeed no two maps, like individuals, are the same.

Even if a group of people are all paying attention to the same external event, their 'perceptual filters', life experiences and collections of different maps and ways of creating maps will ensure that the event is interpreted in many distinctive and varied ways (O'Connor, 2001). This process is called deletion, distortion and generalising (Jacobson, 1996; Bandler, 2008b; Silvester, 2009).

Essentially with different interpretations and perceptions (maps) we are functioning with potentially inaccurate information. When making decisions it is important to be aware that this should serve as a reminder to check that as much information has been elicited, by asking the right questions.

How we communicate includes both the surface and the deep structure processes. These would typically involve:

1. An individual has an experience which is assimilated by the five senses.
2. This information is filtered according to the individual's values and beliefs. Information perceived not to be important is deleted and changed to fit with these beliefs and values and, in order to process the volume of information, it is generalised.
3. When this experience is shared with someone else it is further deleted (summarised), distorted and generalised to fit the context and the available 'talk time' and becomes the 'surface structure'.
4. This experience, or story, now becomes an experience for the listener, who absorbs and processes the information (as in 1 and 2 above), with the resultant version of the listener's account stored as deep structure information within the neurology.
5. When the listener shares this version, he or she too will repeat the process identified in 3 above. Further distortion, deletion and generalisation will have occurred as the listener shares this surface structure information. And the process is repeated however many times the story is told.

Language

Everyday language therefore is the process by which we communicate and reflect our map of the world: 'our reality'. Language can reveal what someone is thinking without the person always being consciously aware. It can unveil the 'script' someone is following: the person's rules.

Purposeful language, however, can create awareness, choices and change. Being aware of the distortions, deletions and generalisations (DDGs) in language is a crucial starting point.

ACTIVITY **8.1**

Working from your own map of the world

Close your eyes and imagine being with a friend or a client who says to you 'I am scared!' Notice all the things in your thoughts of what that means. It will include a representation of your friend or client and a picture of him or her being afraid, together with additional information which you have added from your own experiences and thoughts about what may or may not be happening. This exercise demonstrates how you are working from your map of the world and not the other person's.

Altering reality (distortions)

This could be described as the sneaky language pattern that we create naturally. Most people lack the intuition, knowledge, skill or sense to hear and recognise it (Hall, 2001). If individuals do identify a discrepancy they often politely avoid directly challenging it. However, if they use the advanced questioning skills with reverence and honesty the information can be recovered without the individuals being overtly challenging.

Altering reality can help us become creative and build more resources within, to accomplish something. It can equally limit; the danger is when the perception of reality is negative and there is no challenge; this can further compound a limiting belief.

In addition, as Jacobson states, 'Throughout our lives we have been gathering information and making judgements about it, these then become our generalisations about ourselves, other people and the world as a whole' (1996: 59). This process can lead to the reality being distorted and altered. Furthermore, because the language we use influences the internal processing, it can also have an effect on the emotional state and behaviour.

When reality is altered in this way by using the values and belief filters, the motivation to protect these and to be loyal is the driving force (Jacobson, 1996). Interestingly, if individuals have not been challenged, they have no knowledge or insight to question what they value or believe.

Altering reality or distortions are responsible for people's fears, horrors and traumas as well as victim identities (Hall, 2007; Bandler, 2008b). It is how individuals feel about themselves, and what they believe is true regarding who they are and what they are capable of. If these beliefs are restrictive, individuals can deliberately challenge the distortion, which will certainly bring about change in their reality of the world.

It is because of these belief systems that individuals are able to evaluate themselves and their self-worth. Self-esteem that affects confidence and assertiveness comes from beliefs about individuals' perceptions of their internal world and how they value things. Dilts (1999: 211) refers to this process as 'thought viruses', which can in turn lead to limiting beliefs.

Equally, this same system can enable individuals to achieve, push for more and perform better than expected (Churches and Terry, 2010).

Within the language patterns of distortion, we are able to hear people's pain and suffering as well as their joy and pride. These language patterns tend to go unnoticed, because the reference is from people's internal representations of themselves and their experience, which are values and belief based. It is a subjective opinion and, rather than challenge the statements which we hear, we tend to accept them.

Distorting and distortions in language patterns can take many forms: mind reading is one example.

Mind reading

There is a belief on the part of the speaker that one person can know what another is thinking and feeling, without a direct and clear communication from the second person (Lazarus, 2010). This perceived wisdom is created from an unconscious process of collating evidence from the external world, applying previous information (patterns and rules) and in the moment creating a logical internal conclusion.

EXAMPLE

'Everyone in the class thinks that I am clever.'

There is a claim (a distortion) of knowing what other people in the class are thinking.

This declaration of knowing what another person is thinking or feeling can reveal someone's beliefs. If individuals have a low opinion, they may look for evidence and distort what is seen and/or heard to match this feeling; for example, they might interpret someone's behaviour, of perhaps being distracted, as not liking them because they are not good enough, or they will distort the information of what people do or say to match their internal feeling.

One of the things to notice is that when people are mind reading they have little choice of the experience, as they have already decided what the other person is thinking and/or feeling, and they therefore respond on a level of assumption about what the other thinks and feels which is likely to be invalid. They will equally assume that the other also knows how they feel and think about themselves (O'Connor and Seymour, 2002). On a more positive note, people can have an optimistic approach and feel as if they know how things are going to turn out, based on their beliefs of what they think will happen.

EXAMPLE

'I have no doubt that this project is going to be a huge success.'

In a dialogue it may look something like this:

Individual:	'She thinks that I am stupid and inadequate.'
Social worker:	'How do you know that?'
Individual:	'She tells me how to do things.'
Social worker:	'What things specifically?'
Individual:	'Things about cooking.'
Social worker:	'Specifically what about cooking?'
Individual:	'Cooking my greens.'

Table 8.1 Examples of how to address mind reading

Statement	Appropriate challenge
'Everyone thinks that I am no good.'	'How specifically do you know they think that?'
'I know what he wants.'	'How do you know what he wants?'
'He thinks that I am stupid.'	'How do you know he thinks that?'
'My boss does not like me.'	'How do you know that she does not like you?'
'I know what you are imagining.'	'How do you know what I am imagining?'

ACTIVITY **8.2**

Mind reading

Identify from the sentences below which contain mind reading language patterns:

1. *Sally does not like me.*
2. *She completed the report.*
3. *I could see that she felt great.*
4. *I know how to make him more receptive.*
5. *The coach detailed the positives.*
6. *I understand your thinking.*
7. *I know what you are feeling.*
8. *He showed me what annoys him.*
9. *I can see how scared they were.*

Less obvious ones are:

10. *If he believed in me, he would demonstrate this.*
11. *I am dismayed that you did not take my position into account.*
12. *You think only of yourself and never of anyone else's feelings.*

There is a cause to my effect (distortion)

This is where the responsibility of someone's state is determined by an outside representation (something or someone outside creates a feeling in me). The client 'X' feels as if he or she has no choice about feeling what he or she is feeling because 'Y' forced 'X' to feel in that particular way. 'X' will see and hear something in the external world and internally translate it to him- or herself from a feeling perspective (Silvester, 2009). Wake (2010: 24) describes this as being at the 'effect of the situation' and therefore passive or not in control.

Alternative words or classification: Cause and effect (Bandler, 2008b: 313).

Depending on the experience this can lead to individuals feeling bad and victims to the external world (the event). This potential powerlessness is created because the individuals perceive they are not the 'cause' of the event and are, therefore, not in control. This distortion can create the perception that the individuals have no choice but to respond in the way they are doing. In contrast, Wake (2010: 24) describes taking control as 'being at cause', which is more powerful and provides the words individuals may use shown in Table 8.2.

In an example, the statement would look something like this:

Y causes **X** to feel some emotion.
'He (**Y**) makes me (**X**) feel sad.'
'My daughter (**Y**) makes me (**X**) feel happy.'
'My wife (**Y**) makes me (**X**) feel angry.'
'Your (**Y**) teasing irritates me (**X**).'

Table 8.3 shows examples of how to challenge these statements appropriately.

Table 8.2 Cause and effect words

Cause	Effect
Responsibility	Reasons
Empowered	Excuses
Ownership	Justifications
'Yes'	'Yes, but'
'I can'	'It's the . . .'

Table 8.3 Examples of how to address cause and effect

Statement	Appropriate challenge
'He makes me sad.'	How does he make you sad?
	How does he sadden you?
'She makes me feel angry.'	How does she make you angry?
	How does she anger you?

ACTIVITY *8.3*

Cause and effect

Write down ten sentences that demonstrate the cause and effect, and identify the 'cause'. For example:

He makes me sad.

> His behaviour is the cause of her feeling sad. The specific behaviour is that he does not help with the shopping.

The sound of that makes me feel insecure.

> What she heard, which caused the insecurity, was that her job is at risk.

Linking one to another (distortion)

This is where two sentences are linked: X is true and therefore Y must also be true. If you isolate the sentences they will appear to be the same or equal to each other. In reality, however, these sentences may be totally unrelated (O'Connor and Seymour, 2002).

Alternative words or classification: Complex equivalence (Bandler, 2008b: 313).

Linking new concepts to established or old knowledge is part of the recognised learning process. However, making the wrong links can have an impact on how resourceful or otherwise an individual feels.

Typically, distortions will relay one surface structure, and cause and then convey another. Characteristically, the two sentences have the same syntactic form. The person is claiming knowledge that is 'mind reading' in the first structure and what is visible to him or her, like smiling or not smiling, in the second, which doesn't require any knowledge of the other person's inner state.

Both structures are generalisations that can be challenged (O'Connor and Seymour, 2002). By checking if the two structures are in fact equal, we can test the distortion. One part of the phrase often exists in 'the world out there' and is true, and the second does not; instead, the significance of the meaning to act is something constructed by the individual and therefore is distorted (Hall, 2001). In simple terms it can be described as jumping to the wrong conclusion. By finding one counter-example, we are able to expose and maybe dispel this pattern.

EXAMPLE

Junior: *The boss is in a bad mood; he is pacing in his office.*
Manager: *Does pacing always mean he is in a bad mood?*
Junior: *I think so.*
Manager: *If you were pacing would that mean that you were in a bad mood?*
Junior: *No, it could mean lots of things.*
Manager: *So do you still think he is in a bad mood?*
Junior: *No.*

ACTIVITY *8.4*

Linking one to another

Write down ten sentences that demonstrate linking one to another patterns (complex equivalence) and also identify a suitable challenge. For example:

'This is difficult. I can't do it.'
If I couldn't do that would it mean that I would find it difficult?
If it was easy would that mean you could do it?

'I can't study. I have older parents to care for.'
If I had older parents, would that mean that I couldn't study?

Table 8.4 Examples of how to address linking one to another patterns

Statement	Appropriate question
'You don't care about me any more; you don't come to see me.'	By not visiting, how does that mean that I don't care about you? If you don't visit me does that mean you don't care about me?
'You are very intelligent; you read many books.'	By reading many books how does that mean I am intelligent? If you read many books would that mean you are intelligent?
'You think you are better than me; you get better responses.'	By getting better responses, how does that mean I am better than you? If you were clever would that mean you are better than me?
'My team leader never appreciates me; he never smiles at me.'	How does him not smiling at you mean that he does not appreciate you? If you were not smiling at him, would that mean you don't appreciate him?

Verb to noun (distortions)

This is where a process word or verb, in deep structure, appears as an event word or noun in the surface structure. Nominalisation is the process of turning a verb or an adjective into a noun. The following discussion will concentrate on the former, verb to noun.

Alternative words or classification: Nominalisation (Bandler, 2008b: 312).

Nouns are persons, places and things. Naming an action as a noun distorts the meaning and, as a result, it sends false signals to our brain–body system (Bandler, 2008b). The false signal is that we represent the word as a non-action rather than as an action. The word is 'frozen' and does not offer resolutions. When this happens, the individual will feel 'stuck' and with limited choices (O'Connor and Seymour, 2002).

The reality is that the words being described don't actually exist apart from by way of association in the mind; they are not tangible. We talk about them as if they are things, when in fact they are activities. They are hidden by the noun-like term (O'Connor and Seymour, 2002).

We leave the problem as if there is no resolution, and this prevents us from identifying a realistic solution. This process makes our problems become 'things'. It is individuals' paradigms of the problem that keep them 'stuck': they are unable to see, hear or feel what specifically is going on and, therefore, cannot find an appropriate solution.

Nominalised words often take on an 'ance', 'ion' or 'ment'. For example:

	Nominalised to
maintain	maintenance
compare	comparison
assess	assessment

move	movement
reduce	reduction
act	action
conclude	conclusion
satisfy	satisfaction
react	reaction
determine	determination

In writing, nominalised sentences are vague, and the readability is reduced. The fewer nominalised words there are, the more succinct and easier information is to read. For example:

'Our discussion concerned the service user's problems'

becomes

'We discussed the service user's problems.'

'This paper provides a comparison of the problems'

becomes

'This paper compares the problems.'

Avoiding nominalisations in writing will make your sentences more succinct and powerful. It will also reduce misunderstandings due to the vagueness.

The following are additional examples of nominalisation:

Nominalisation	De-nominalisation
success	succeed
fear	fearing
discussion	discuss
decision	decide
embarrassment	embarrass
communication	communicate
relationship	relate
excitement	exciting
education	educate
relaxation	relaxing
frustration	frustrate
satisfaction	satisfy
investigation	investigate

To resolve these, the first thing to do is to recognise them by asking if the word can fit into a 'wheelbarrow' (O'Connor and Seymour, 2002).

Imagine this:

1. I want to have a desk.
2. I want to have confidence.

You could imagine putting a desk in a mental wheelbarrow. However, the word 'confidence' (or any of the above nominalisation words) cannot be put in a wheelbarrow. It makes no sense. Or you could use the phrase 'an ongoing _____'. True nouns like 'chair', 'desk' or 'door' don't fit into the blank part of the phrase; for example, an 'ongoing chair' is nonsense. Another example: an 'ongoing chair' versus an 'ongoing decision'.

A final test is the opposite test, for each nominalisation has an opposite. For example, the opposite of 'empowerment' is 'disempowerment', whereas there is no opposite of 'car'. To solve this, we change the nouns back into event words, back into ongoing processes; this helps the client to identify new choices and decisions. Usually with these sentences there is also deletion, and it is important to recognise both.

Table 8.5 Examples of how to address verb to noun patterns

Statement	Appropriate challenge
'I have no confidence in leading a team.'	What would leading your team confidently feel like?
'I have a fear of presenting.'	What are you fearing most about presenting?
'I want to communicate better.'	What would better communicating sound, look and feel like?

ACTIVITY *8.5*

Nominalisations and their verb counterparts

List ten nominalisations and identify their verb counterparts.

Value statement (distortions)

This is where a statement or an opinion, which is based usually on a value or belief, is presented as a fact, when the original person making this judgement or the evidence on which the judgement is made is missing. It is therefore an unsupported statement.

Alternative words or classification: Lost performative (Bandler, 2008b: 313).

For example: 'Clearly it is wrong to be late.'

In whose opinion is it wrong to be late? The main performer making the claim is not mentioned. Value statements function as rules, with no reference, and people in general assume them to be true (O'Connor and Seymour, 2002).

In organisations, the statement 'We've always done it this way' would be a good example. Table 8.6 provides examples and appropriate challenges.

ACTIVITY *8.6*

Value statements

List ten value statements and identify an appropriate challenge for each.

Table 8.6 Examples of how to address value statements

Statement	Appropriate challenge
'It's wrong to challenge the group.'	Wrong for whom?
'This is the way we should do it.'	Do it for whom?
'He's acting strangely.'	According to whom?
'It's not good to be late.'	According to whom?
'Mistakes have been made.'	According to whom? Specifically what mistakes?
'Nobody is pulling their weight.'	According to whom?
'She is more flexible these days.'	According to whom?
'People say it's wrong to do that.'	Which people? According to whom?

Summary of questions to ask when there are distortions caused by the individual making statements that are not backed up by evidence

According to whom?
Who says that?
How do you know . . .?
How does X = Y? If X is true, Y must also be true.
Can I ask how specifically?

Leaving out or omitting information (deletions)

We learnt earlier that there is a reason why we delete information, and that is simply to manage the vast quantities of data. There is also a process of representing the world twice: firstly, taking in information consciously (seven plus or minus two elements) and unconsciously, categorising it according to previous experience, beliefs and values and then, secondly, re-presenting it in the form of words and non-verbal gestures. These two processes can each delete crucial information intentionally or unintentionally. This 'transformation' of what is in the 'deep structure' to the surface of what is presented either verbally or in writing is therefore altered.

The purpose of recognising deletions is to assist individuals in restoring a fuller representation of their experience to attain clarity and, with it, greater choices and resourcefulness. A deletion is a process which removes part of the original information and creates an impoverished representation. It has benefits in terms of stopping individuals from becoming overwhelmed and overloaded with stimuli and information. Indeed, Hall (2001) agrees that not all deletions create problems. We also know that the brain can suppress and learn to block information such as painful or unwanted memories (Anderson et al., 2004; Sample, 2007).

However, it can also be counterproductive if important resourceful materials have been deleted. O'Connor (2001: 134) would describe them as the result of a linguistic 'blind spot'. Deletions, by nature, suggest that an individual is not clear, for there is a lack of specificity.

Being a great communicator is all about being able to hear the deletions and, if necessary, recover the information by using the meta-model, advanced questioning skills. Below are descriptions of the different types of deletions and examples of appropriate questions to challenge and elicit the missing information.

Basic (simple deletion)

These are very simple breaches in language structure and are often short sentences with missing words or details. The information is too general, and there is vital material omitted, making it difficult to understand the statement, unless your own references are added; an obvious misinterpretation may be the result.

To identify a deletion, simply ask: 'What has to be true for the sentence to make sense, and what information is missing?' or 'What question can I ask to get that information?' Fortunately, most people with or without training will intuitively ask the relevant question to recover the information.

Alternative words or classification: Simple deletion (Bandler, 2008b: 311).

Challenging a simple deletion can elicit the original information or additional details to provide clarity and reduce any misunderstandings.

Table 8.7 Examples of how to address simple deletions

Statement	Appropriate challenge
'You can feel good.'	Feel good about what?
'I am confused.'	What are you confused about?
'It's an interesting thing.'	What is interesting, and how?
'It's quite simple.'	What is simple, and how?
'I wonder if you care.'	Care about what, and how?
'I was told not to do that.'	Told not to do what? By whom?
'You can't.'	Cannot what?
'It's all wrong.'	What is? According to whom?
'I know.'	Know what?
'Service users don't care.'	According to whom? About what? What evidence do you have?

ACTIVITY 8.7

Basic deletions

List ten statements that reflect simple deletion language patterns, and identify appropriate challenges for each.

Compared to what? (deletion)

Again, this language pattern is simple and represented by an element of evaluation. However, the object that something is being compared to is missing. There is a lack of specificity.

Alternative words or classification: Comparative deletions (Bandler, 2008b: 312).

It typically shows up in adjectives and words ending in 'er' ('better') or 'est' ('smartest') or with more ('more significant') or less ('less poignant') (Hall, 2001: 80). 'Worse' or 'worst' are also clue words that a comparison may be being made.

Words like 'obviously' and 'clearly', adverbs ending in 'ly', result in a deletion implicitly the individual making the comparison is missing. For example:

'Clearly this is an excellent project.'

There is also a degree of judgement taking place. If the sentence can be changed to 'It is clear . . .' then there is a deletion (O'Connor 2001: 95). According to Hall (2001: 81), what is deleted is often the measure by which an individual is making the comparison, the internal standards. For example, in 'She is the best boss' the information about best compared to whom and the details of how are missing. Another example is:

'I am the worst report writer.'

Internal high standards can create unrealistic comparisons, and often the deleted element is just as 'unrealistic', but left unchallenged such a comparison is a proverbial rod to beat oneself or others with, and is limiting.

You will hear words like:

Than	Much
Worse than	Fewer
More	Faster
Less	Slower
Unfortunately	Smarter
Surprisingly	Better
Higher	Too
Lower	Best
Even	Greater

The statements in Table 8.8 are examples.

Table 8.8 Examples of how to address 'compared to what?' deletions

Statement	Appropriate challenge
'He is better at risk management.'	Better than whom?
'This is worse than I anticipated.'	Worse than what?
'He earns more.'	More than whom?
'He prefers his approach.'	In comparison to what or whom?
'You are too inappropriate.'	Too inappropriate in comparison to what or whom?
'The results have been better.'	Compared with what?
'They look more at ease.'	More at ease than when?
'This is far more effective.'	More effective than what?
'I presented badly in court.'	Compared to whom? Badly compared to what?

ACTIVITY 8.8

'*Compared to what?' language patterns*

List ten sentences that reflect 'compared to what?' language patterns and identify an appropriate challenge.

Unclear verb (deletion)

In this case the verb word is unspecified. The verb normally describes what occurs, the movement and actions in a sentence. If there is insufficient information with regard to what is happening to the verb, the 'author or agent of an action is unclear' (Bandler, 2008b: 312), and the individual is left surmising, guessing and filling in the gaps. To some degree all verbs are unspecified.

Alternative words or classification: Unspecified verb (Bandler, 2008b: 312).

Hall (2001) agrees that this form of deletion leads to individuals inventing meanings rather than getting the information from the original speaker. So listen to the individual's surface structure, identifying the process words or verbs, and ask yourself whether the image presented is clear enough for you to imagine the actual sequence of events as they are being described.

If you find that there are gaps then the verb is insufficiently specific and you need to ask for more information. The questions to elicit the missing information would typically start with 'what', 'when', 'where', 'how' and 'who(m)' followed by 'specifically'. This lack of detail may not always cause a problem, and there may be no need to elicit further information.

Molden (2001: 108) suggests that the following words are typical examples: 'going', 'performing', 'managing' and 'leading'. Each describes little about the activity, the what or the how. For example:

'He's performing badly.'
'She's leading poorly.'

These two statements could be challenged by asking 'how specifically' he or she is performing badly or leading poorly. This information is important in understanding how this situation can be improved or rectified.

Table 8.9 Examples of how to address unclear verbs

Statement	Appropriate challenge
'He upset me.'	How specifically did he upset you?
'He cycles to the office.'	How did he cycle to the office?
'He likes her.'	How specifically does he like her?
'He wrote the letter.'	How specifically did he write the letter?
'He typed the report incorrectly.'	How specifically did he do that?
	How did he type it incorrectly?
'I told her, now she should do it correctly.'	What specifically did you tell her?
'I calmed the family down.'	How specifically?
'She always falls.'	When, how or where specifically?

ACTIVITY 8.9

Unclear verbs

List ten statements that reflect unclear verb language patterns, and identify an appropriate challenge.

Unclear noun or pronoun (deletion)

In this language structure what is lacking is anything specific about the noun or pronoun. This can lead to insufficient information detailing the individual's experience or a failure to specify who is the agent or object of an action.

Alternative words or classification: Lack of referential index (Bandler, 2008b: 320).

It may or may not be relevant to gather the missing information. If the speaker is being unspecific and it is not causing a problem, there is no need to elicit additional information. However, if the statements are vague or unfocused then more detailed information may be required and can be elicited by asking 'Who or what specifically?'

Often people use 'they' and 'it', particularly in organisations, to refer to the senior management. This type of deletion can be unhelpful, potentially implying that an individual is helpless and unable to have an impact or change the situation.

For example:

'They never listen to us.'
'They decide how it is going to be.'

'Who specifically?' and 'What specifically?' are appropriate challenges for both of these statements. Other clues to the presence of 'unclear nouns' would be the use of words like 'we', 'a person', 'someone' and 'people'.

Omitting nouns can also make sentences impersonal. For example:

'The project was completed.'

A lack of ownership may also be implied.

Table 8.10 Examples of how to address unclear nouns or pronouns

Statement	Appropriate challenge
'People are resourceful.'	Who specifically is resourceful?
'Nobody listens to me.'	Who specifically doesn't listen to you?
'This is easy to do.'	What specifically is easy to do?
'I love writing this.'	What specifically do you like about writing?
'They should know better.'	Better than whom?
'The writing is on the wall.'	For whom? According to whom?

ACTIVITY 8.10

Unclear nouns or pronouns

List ten sentences which contain unclear nouns or pronouns, and identify an appropriate challenge for each.

Summary of questions to ask when there are deletions in someone's speech

What, who(m), when, where or how (specifically)?

Generalising – all the same

It is characteristic of humans to generalise information and knowledge to assimilate data and learn. Experiences are grouped and categorised from childhood to make sense of the world quickly and to avoid relearning, but in the process some of the fuller details are lost from the original experience.

This essential reduction and deficit of information can impoverish an individual's thinking, as exceptions to the 'learnt rules', for example that all trees are green and all skies are blue, can be missed. In addition, someone might frequently generalise or mistakenly generalise; for example, someone who thinks 'I had a bad meeting experience with a headteacher' might conclude that all headteachers are the same and all future meetings with them will be difficult. Taking one example and categorising in this way to produce broad conclusions is generalising. 'All or nothing' thinking can be representative of extreme generalising.

The beliefs we hold on to as 'truth' are generalisations, which serve to predict and act as operating principles. Individuals also identify and look for instances and information to support these 'beliefs' and ignore data which may question them.

This can prevent individuals from utilising a fuller set of choices in coping with any particular situation, or seeing what has been missed and generalised out of the proverbial picture. The purpose of identifying generalisations is to reconnect them to the original experience, reduce obstacles and ensure that detail and richness are present. One way to determine this is to identify certain words and phrases in the client's surface structure, or what is said, which are non-process words or nouns that are unspecified (Bandler, 2008b).

All is judged the same (universal quantifiers)

Quantifying a statement with the same measure, generalising a few instances to represent the whole, and judging all to be the same are uses of a universal quantifier. When this pattern is used it gives the impression of certainty and assertiveness, even if for the speaker this was the first experience. It also makes the world a simple place, as all specific details are removed (O'Connor and Seymour, 2002). It's 'black and white', and typically you will hear the use of the following words: 'never', 'always', 'ever', 'each', 'all', 'every', 'nothing', 'nobody', 'none' and 'nowhere'. O'Connor and Seymour (2002: 99) describe generalisations as 'linguistic fluff that clogs the works of clear communication'.

Alternative words or classification: Generalisations, for example universal quantifiers (Bandler, 2008b: 314).

EXAMPLE

- *'Everyone will think I am stupid, starting my Master's when I am so busy.'*
- *'I never get this right!'*
- *'I fail every time I try this.'*
- *'You can't trust anyone.'*

Often, though, there is implied generalisation without the obvious words; these can be detected by noticing the exaggeration in the sentence.

EXAMPLE

'People push me around.'

The noun 'people' carries no referential index (the people are not specified in terms of 'who') and therefore fails to identify anything specific. The word 'people' becomes too generalised and now refers to all people. The speaker is being mistreated by the entire planet.

EXAMPLE

'My friend pushes me around.'

The sentence contains two nouns, both bearing a referential index, and so the first thing is to identify each non-process word and then ask if it picks up a specific person or subject. If it fails to pick up a specific person or subject then there is a generalisation. Not knowing whom or what someone is referring to can lead to misunderstandings. Unchallenged, these generalisations become accepted as fact.

Once an 'all is judged the same' generalisation is identified, a 'who' or 'what' question will help to establish the missing information, thus assisting the individual to reconnect the generalisation to the experience. Assigning referential indices will help reduce the generalisation and adds richness and details back to the individual's model. Once successfully challenged, the generalisation no longer holds true.

Table 8.11 Generalisations – statements and explanations

Statement	Explanation
'Nobody pays any attention to what I say.'	'Nobody' and 'what' have no referential index or subject.
'I saw my best friend.'	All nouns have indices.
'Let us not get lost in the plot.'	'Us' and 'plot' have no indices.
'One should respect another's feelings.'	'One' and 'another' have no indices.

EXAMPLE

Junior: *I am scared of starting my degree; everyone will think I am stupid.*
Manager: *Everyone in the whole world?*
Junior: *No, my family and friends.*

Manager: *Who specifically will think you are stupid?*
Junior: *My brothers and ex-husband.*
Manager: *All your brothers and ex-husband?*
Junior: *No, just two of them and the ex.*
Manager: *Do you care about their opinion?*
Junior: *Not at all.*
Manager: *Do you still think that they will think that you are stupid?*
Junior: *No, not at all. Actually, I don't care much about their opinion.*

EXAMPLE

Junior: *Nobody pays any attention to what I say!*
Manager: *Who specifically doesn't pay attention to you?*
Junior: *Well, certain people at certain times don't pay attention to me.*
Manager: *Do you know the reason that they don't?*
Junior: *No, not really.*
Manager: *What could be a reason?*
Junior: *They don't like me.*
Manager: *What else?*
Junior: *They are busy.*
Manager: *Is it possible that this could be the reason?*
Junior: *Yes, I see what you mean.*

ACTIVITY *8.11*

Universal quantifiers

List ten statements that reflect the universal quantifier (all is judged to be the same) language pattern, and identify an appropriate challenge for each.

Mood controllers (generalisation)

These are words that modify the mood of the main verb in a sentence. They are the linguistic reflections of belief and judgement and set the 'unspoken rules' or principles, typically of desire, choice, necessity, impossibility or possibility (O'Connor, 2001: 96).

Alternative words or classification: Modal operators (Bandler, 2008b: 319).

This group of words, because they are based on beliefs and internal rules, behave like filters in the language structure and therefore create generalisations. Hall (2001: 90) describes them as depicting a person's 'mode or state' of operating in the world, for individuals have their preferred 'mood words' which provide clues to their 'state' and can be identified verbally or in writing.

There are two main mood operators:

1. necessity;
2. possibility.

EXAMPLE

Necessity:

> *'I can't speak in public.'*
> *'I have to write the report.'*
> *'I need to finish this.'*

Possibility:

> *'I might tell them now.'*
> *'I could finish the document.'*
> *'I may phone later.'*

When reading each of the above statements you can hear the mood of the sentence. Of particular note is that, no matter what the verb is, it will still create the same mood. Interestingly, some of the above words used may instantly resonate, while others may feel more awkward.

As linguistic reflections of belief the words can operate in two differing ways, providing limiting or less useful parameters, for example 'should', 'must' and 'have to', which are controllers of necessity, and 'can', 'could' and 'want', which are controllers of possibility.

Churches and Terry (2010) suggest that words of 'necessity' can also be used to delete significant amounts of information to qualify a point of view. They operate by referring to past stances, for example 'We must do it like this.' Equally, modal operators enhance people's ability to make good decisions and motivate themselves. Challenging the modal operator, if it is of 'necessity', will reveal some of the limiting beliefs that people may have about the subject. See in what sequence people use their 'mood' controllers, and mirror them back.

Observe the submodalities and how they change as the mood operator is changed. Notice that people who will not negotiate 'their needs' may negotiate and exchange some of 'their wants' with some of 'their likes', as they are more accommodating with wants and likes.

According to Hall (2001), with a modal operator of necessity the consequence has been deleted. For example, an appropriate challenge to 'I need to' would be 'Or else?' or 'What will happen if you don't?'

'Mood operators', particularly those of necessity, can dominate the internal dialogue, or self-talk: 'You need to', 'You must.' Developed when we were children, copied maybe from worried parents or through school experiences, they can continue to be used daily throughout life, even if they are limiting.

In language you can challenge anyone's limiting mood controllers by changing the tense to the past. If you use the past tense you are no longer in the present. The challenge 'What would happen if you didn't?' is very useful. Asking someone 'What stops you?', particularly when the person uses the word 'can't', suggests the possibility that the person 'can' and that there is an alternative way of looking at something, and with it more flexibility and choice.

When someone says they 'can' do something, a modal operator of possibility, this is not usually limiting and therefore does not require challenging (O'Connor, 2001).

A note about 'contingency'

Modal operators of 'contingency' include words like 'might', 'could', 'would', 'would like', 'wish' and 'maybe'. These modal operators are about considering something that may be beyond what is perceived to be possible – possible but not very likely.

They can link with the modal operator of possibility, for example 'a wish', once perceived and given credibility that it can become tangible, becomes 'possible' and, once possible, by means of the modal operator of 'necessity' potentially becomes realised.

EXAMPLE

'I would love to be able to . . .' (contingency).
'I know I am capable of . . .' (possibility).
'And so I should have a go' (necessity).

Table 8.12 shows typical words that are mood controllers.

Table 8.12 Typical words that are mood controllers

Possibility	Necessity (indicates a lack of choice)
Able	Have to
Can	Need to
Want	Must
Could	Mustn't
Wish	Should
May	Shouldn't
Get to	Couldn't
Will	Ought to
Choose	Can't
Desire	Got to
Capable	Expected to
	Supposed to

Contingency	Qualifiers
Might	I really need to . . .
Would	I just want to . . .
Wouldn't	I jolly well ought to . . .
Could	I absolutely must . . .

ACTIVITY *8.12*

Experiment with mood controllers

Think of something that you thought you couldn't do. Now try all the other modal operators (see Table 8.12) and notice if you feel differently about that particular thing.

'I must work' could possibly conjure up a feeling of lethargy. Changing it to 'I want to work' will change the mood and create a sense of choice.

Experiment with the behaviours that don't inspire you, and try on the mood controllers of the behaviours that do inspire you (use some of the words in Table 8.12 and notice the difference).

ACTIVITY *8.13*

Limiting and motivating mood controllers

Think of something that you should do and notice how you feel. Next think of something that you shouldn't do and notice how you feel. Think of something you'd love to do and notice what modal operator you would use. Now use this modal operator when talking about something you don't feel motivated to do.

Identify the mood operators that limit you and those that motivate you. Change your limiting ones to motivating ones and notice if there is a difference in how you feel.

- *Write three sentences using mood controllers to imply something different for the listener to consider.*
- *Write three sentences using mood controllers to imply why someone should consider working with you.*

What is assumed? (generalisation)

Every sentence in order to work has to have some basic assumptions that certain things within the sentence are true for it to be logical and understandable. However, sometimes we assume too much and distort what is there, adding and therefore changing the meaning of sentences to what is presumed to have been said and meant.

Alternative words or classification: Presuppositions (Bandler, 2008b: 318).

When some information is missing, the unconscious fills in the gaps to make sense. Part of this labelling process involves judging.

O'Connor and Seymour (2002: 102) would suggest that basic assumptions that 'limit choice' may need to be challenged. They propose that these are often disguised or hidden as 'why questions'. For example, 'Why can't you take care of me properly?' presupposes that the person is not being properly taken care of, and any response would be inadequate, thus confirming the presupposition. Other examples could include:

- 'Why can't you do anything right?'
- 'Why are you so difficult?'

It is important to be able to identify these generalisations in order to establish what is presupposed in an individual's language, and to identify any limiting patterns or assumptions. The advanced questioning techniques described within this section can be used to reveal what is being presupposed.

The words 'since', 'if' and 'when' in a sentence often denote that there is a presupposition (O'Connor and Seymour, 2002: 102). In addition, anything following verbs such as 'realise', 'know' and 'ignore' frames a presupposition (Hall, 2001: 128), for example 'realise why we place so much importance on the individual' (O'Connor and Seymour, 2002: 102).

Listening for the assumptions is one of the most powerful techniques that an individual can learn in order to better appreciate what questions are required to elicit the missing information or to challenge what is presupposed if it is restrictive. Good communicators are able to 'be present' with a clear mind, aware and curious about what is being communicated.

O'Connor (2001) reports that any presupposition that is 'limiting of choice, thought and action' should be challenged, and provides the following examples:

Statement	Presupposition
'How many times must I tell you before you'll stop doing that?'	'I'll have to tell you a number of times before you will stop.'
'When will you act responsibly?'	'You are not acting responsibly now.'
'How bad can this get?'	'It's bad now.'
'I don't like the way you ignore me.'	'You ignore me.'
'When will you discuss the service agreement?'	'We will discuss the service agreement.'

Presuppositions can be appropriately exposed and challenged by asking, for example, 'What leads you to believe . . .?' The remainder of the sentence will reveal what is presupposed.

Another example is illustrated in the description that follows:

Ivan left town, leaving behind a trail of destruction.

Reading this sentence, what can we assume is true?

- There is someone or something called Ivan.
- There is a town.
- Ivan left town.
- There was a trail of destruction.

Anything else that we assume, we actually don't know, for example:

- Ivan is a man.
- Ivan caused the destruction.

When we look at what is assumed, we are able to know what to ask in order to retrieve more information and clarify what is meant. All sentences have missing information or are altered from the real event and generalised. Most of the time it is not a problem; however, when we examine the assumptions we are able to decide whether more information is required or not. The question is: what assumptions or presuppositions are you accepting in your daily conversations?

There is an important emphasis in terms of using positive presuppositions as guiding principles. Within NLP there are a group of accepted fundamental presuppositions which act as important values and principles upon which NLP is and should be practised. These provide a solid foundation, code of practice and fundamental starting point; a list of these can be found in Appendix 2.

You will learn more about specific presuppositions representative of the Milton language patterns in the next section.

Summary of questions to ask when there are generalisations

What are the assumptions and mood of the sentence, and is the individual using words like:

- Always and never?
- Nobody? Always? Everyone? All?
- Can't?
- So what would happen if?
- What stops you?

    What is being presupposed?

The special case of 'why'

A number of authors recommend using the 'why question' with extreme caution (O'Connor and Lages, 2004; Churches and Terry, 2010; Whitmore, 2010). Churches and Terry (2010: 125), for example, suggest that 'why' is a word which 'requires us to look back to the past'. This type of question can also be interrogating, as it challenges someone to understand the motivation, creating potentially a defensive stance.

There is a degree of implied justification and judgement which can create resistance. Churches and Terry (2010: 125) recommend not using the why question particularly in relation to 'behaviour and competence'. Youell and Youell (2011: 98) would instead advise asking:

'And what's important about . . .?'

Table 8.13 summarises all the different advanced questioning skills (meta-model) language patterns.

Table 8.13 Summary of advanced questioning skills

Pattern	Description	Classification	Challenge
Distortions	Altering reality	Mind reading	How do you know?
	Cause to my effect	Cause and effect	How specifically?
	Linking one to another	Complex equivalents	If I did X would that mean that I couldn't do Y?
	Verb to noun	Nominalisation	How do you have to behave?
	Value statement	Lost performative	According to whom?
Generalisations	All judged the same	Universal quantifiers	Who specifically?
	Mood controllers	Modal operators	What would happen if you decided not to?

Table 8.13 Continued

Pattern	Description	Classification	Challenge
	What is assumed	Presuppositions	
Deletions	Basic	Simple	What, when, where, how, who?
	Compared to what?	Comparative	In comparison to whom or what?
	Unclear verb	Unspecified verbs	What or how specifically?
	Unclear noun or pronoun	Lack of referential index	Who or what?

TIPS FOR SUCCESS

Understanding linguistics is very powerful, particularly in reducing misunderstandings and challenging limiting thoughts. Some authors would suggest that if you want to change the results in your life you need to change the language used (McMaster and Grinder, 1993; Jacobson, 1996; Dilts, 1999; Hall, 2001; Bandler, 2008b).

There are a myriad of important leadership roles and scenarios where this advanced questioning knowledge would be useful and crucial. The following are just a few examples you can engage:

- *Lead and manage changes through others.*
- *Challenge assumptions and negotiate with individuals.*
- *Be competent in creating and maintaining purposeful networks and collaborative relationships.*
- *Critically evaluate arguments, assumptions and data to make judgements, take decisions and identify appropriate solutions.*
- *Reflect on practice and challenge your own thinking.*
- *Hold people to account by setting clear targets and direction.*
- *Identify risks by checking assumptions.*
- *Develop productive working relationships with colleagues by reducing misunderstandings.*
- *Manage a project by being very clear, challenging any incorrect presumptions.*
- *Identify and clearly communicate policy directives matched to the individual's representational preferences; this could be for the public or other staff.*
- *Resolve customer service problems through creating clarity, particularly by eliciting the 'deep structure'.*

Indeed, Blanchard (2007: 215) suggests that the reason why individuals resist change is because their concerns regarding a change are not 'surfaced or addressed'. In addition, as Rose Charvet (1997) would emphasise, it is so very effective to be able to predict a person's behaviours by what they say and, importantly, how language can also influence and motivate an individual.

Part 3

Effective influencing and motivating others

Section 9
Persuasive language

Persuasive language is about getting people to believe that they have the resources required to achieve and be effective, which is essential for motivating individuals and teams. The impact can be charismatic.

Empowering beliefs for creating change is about recognising that all individuals have their own view of the world, described in Section 8 as a 'map', and therefore their own interpretation of events and experiences. Respecting and understanding these differences, and the principle that the actions of an individual are not the same as who that person is, create the foundation for effective communication.

A compelling and very skilled communicator, Milton H. Erickson, has been described as one of the most significant individuals who demonstrated 'highly skilled and effective use of language' (Linder-Pelz, 2010: 91). He had a profound effect on Richard Bandler and John Grinder, co-founders of NLP, who modelled Erickson in the early 1970s and then published several books which demonstrated the language patterns they had noted. These formed the basis of the 'Milton model'.

Erickson connected with people's reality, describing what they must have experienced, and leading them to new ways of creating behavioural change. He instinctively was exquisite at rapport building, both verbally and non-verbally. He believed that the clients had the resources within to make any necessary changes, and he helped them to access these (Bandler and Grinder, 1975b).

Reverse of the meta-model (advanced questioning)

Part of the Milton model is called the reverse of the meta-model, as the meta is very precise and the Milton is 'artfully vague' (Molden, 2007: 136) and involves abstract language. Both models use the same language patterns.

The meta-model is applied to elicit more information and to identify the linguistic patterns used to determine what has been deleted, generalised and distorted. The same language patterns using the Milton model can create ambiguity and vagueness, with the intention of following the way the 'mind works' to encourage individuals to make sense and create greater choices in overcoming difficulties or perceived problems (O'Connor and Seymour, 2002: 114). This model helps individuals to use their creative imagination, access their own resources and produce new ways of thinking and behaving.

The meta-model therefore provides approaches to recover specific details from the 'deep structure', information deleted by clients in their speech, the 'surface structure'. The Milton model presents opportunities to construct sentences with almost all specific material missing. This is purposeful, for vague or ambiguous language creates an opportunity to search within for meaning. This requires listeners to fill in the deletions from their own individual experiences, and thoughts creating a unique and personal encounter with the necessary changes in behaviour are more likely to occur. Remember, tapping into someone else's map of reality, and getting the person to use his or her own words, is far more powerful than any other mechanism for bringing about change.

'Chunking up language'

This model, in NLP terms, 'chunks' language 'up' rather than 'down' (as in the case of the meta-model) (O'Connor, 2001: 205). 'Chunking up' creates generalisations, distortions and deletions, which allows access to the unconscious resources and moves individuals away from being lost in the detail to being able to identify for themselves meaning which resonates. 'Chunking down', in contrast, elicits information which may have been deleted, distorted and generalised.

According to Wake, 'Behaviours are driven by our unconscious mind therefore any communication that facilitates direct communication to the unconscious is more likely to influence change than the more conscious dialogue' (2010: 120).

The following examples of language patterns in the Milton model are grouped in the same way as in the meta-model as distortions, deletions and generalisations. The definitions detailed in Section 8 can therefore be applied. The first distortion language pattern to be examined is 'mind reading'.

Distortions

1. Altering reality (mind reading)

Mind reading in persuasive language (Milton model) can be very effective in building credibility and rapport (Bandler and Grinder, 1975b). The following are examples of this language pattern in use:

'I wonder what you're feeling?'	Suggests that the person is feeling something.
'You're curious about the outcomes.'	How do you know the person is curious?
'I know that you have experienced confidence.'	How do you know?
'We both know how important this is to you.'	How do we know?
'I know you are becoming more intrigued by the project.'	What makes you think that?

O' Connor (2001: 177) provides the following example: 'You are easily able to make sense of this as you become more curious about exactly what you are going to learn.' This implies a curiosity which will help the individual learn.

If the mind reading is too specific, however, the impact is reduced. The speaker then runs the risk of losing rapport, as the listener is unable fully to use his or her own resources to fill in the gaps. Mind reading is often used in speeches. For example:

- 'I know you've been waiting to hear what the organisation has to say.'
- 'I know that you believe passionately in what you do.'

ACTIVITY **9.1**

Mind reading persuasive language patterns

- *Write three sentences using mind reading persuasive language patterns to build some credibility for a new behaviour.*
- *Write three sentences using mind reading persuasive language patterns to help someone decide to use your services.*

---

2. Cause to my effect (cause and effect)

This language pattern implies that 'one thing causes another' (Wake 2010: 121). It is classically used to blame or to not take responsibility: 'X caused this.' The statement might be untrue, or there may also be no direct link between the one thing and the other. Using the meta-model (advanced questioning) to explore this is useful if the behaviour or thinking is limiting. However, in the Milton model this language pattern can be used to make positive causal links.

Making causal links, one thing leading to another, is about natural sequencing, and presenting ideas in this format can increase their acceptance. For this to occur one part of the sentence needs to hold true; the second is accepted simply because of the linkage.

The words below are often used:

- if . . . then;
- since;
- so;
- as you . . . then you;
- makes;
- causes.

- because . . . then;
- requires;
- and;
- and that means;
- for;

- during;
- soon;
- as you . . . so you;
- incite;
- produce;

The following are examples of cause and effect statements:

- 'As we contemplate the successes of last year, then we can focus our consideration on the potential further improvements we can make.'
- 'If you can concentrate on this then you can learn many things.'
- 'And knowing that you can gives you every opportunity to change.'
- 'If you can achieve that, then you can reach your targets.'
- 'And if you practise your new skills with your colleagues you will then realise how things can be different.'

Bavister and Vickers suggest using 'negative phrasing', as it is more difficult for the individual to track what is being linked. They provide the following example: 'You won't be able to resist getting more curious as you hear what's coming next' (2004: 192).

3. Linking one to another (complex equivalents)

This is when a suggestion is given that one thing is the same as, or equated to, something else and therefore 'their meanings become equivalent' (Wake, 2010: 123).

The linkage can be created by words like:

- 'That means . . .'
- 'This means . . .'
- 'And therefore . . .'
- 'Then . . .'

Simply using a comma, semi-colon or hyphen can link the two.

EXAMPLE

- *'This means, you are getting all the help you need.'*
- *'Seeing you today, demonstrates you have made a decision.'*
- *'Because you have control – you have a choice in all that you do.'*
- *'Now that you're here today, you will learn well.'*
- *'Being present, means that you will change easily.'*

Complex equivalents can be identified by substituting 'is the same as' for the linking verb, whereas the word 'causes' does not fit.

4. Verb to noun (nominalisation)

This group of language patterns take the place of nouns. They act as nouns, when actually they are frozen verbs. They are not real; they can't be touched and so are not tangible. This process is called nominalisation and, whenever it is used, it denotes that information is distorted.

It can be very effective in allowing speakers to be vague and listeners to search through their own resources and experiences to make sense of the words (O'Connor and Seymour, 2002). See pages 58–60 for further details of this group of language patterns.

EXAMPLE

- *'You are gaining new insights, building new friendships.'*
- *'People can come to new insights.'*
- *'Your communication has been developed.'*
- *'Excitement is part of change.'*
- *'The decision to learn is clear.'*

---

5. Value statements (lost performative)

As in the meta-model there is value judgement or evaluation where the performer or the source of the value is missing. Value statements are indicators of beliefs that individuals hold and most of the time are unconscious about.

Alternative words or classification: Lost performative (Bandler, 2008b: 316).

As the speaker, you can use them to introduce ideas to the listener, which has positive effects without any evidence as to why. Value statements are a good way to deliver pre-suppositions (Molden, 2007). For example, a sentence which starts 'A person is able to . . .' suggests or presupposes possibility that someone can, but the person making the statement is missing; however, this arguably is irrelevant.

Also see page 60 for additional details of this language pattern.

Other examples include:

- 'It is easy to finish the report.' According to whom?
- 'It does not matter how quickly you get used to this.' Who said?
- 'It is a good thing to allow yourself to relax.' According to whom?
- 'No habit can survive the power of the mind.' Who said?

ACTIVITY **9.2**

Using value statements to promote your services

Write three sentences using value statements to promote your services.

Deletions

1. Leaving out (simple or comparative deletions)

The Milton model is used purposefully to delete or omit information so that listeners exercise their own resources to fill in the gaps (Boyes, 2006). In the process the experience becomes unique to the individuals. This can be simple or complex in nature; see also page 62.

For instance, a comparison is made, but the specific details are missing, thus allowing the individual to fill in the deleted information. The following are examples:

- 'And this new way will be so much better.' Better than what?
- 'And I wonder if you are getting curious about what you will experience next?' There is not enough information on what to get curious about.
- 'I know that you are curious.' Again, there is no information provided on what to get curious about.
- 'And just for you . . .' What is just?
- 'It's easy.' Easier than what? In comparison to what?
- 'You will feel more and more able to . . .' The comparison is missing: more able to what, or in comparison to what or when? However, it creates no resistance and is a positive statement.

2. Unclear verb (unspecified verb)

Generally, verbs are unspecified, but sometimes they are more unspecified than they need to be. The verb describes what happens and is the doing part, the movement, or action words in a sentence. Again, speakers use verbs that are more unspecified with a purpose, so that listeners have to search in their own experience to make sense of what is being said, and this then becomes very personal to the individuals (Wake, 2010). Also see page 64 for a supplementary explanation and examples.

Alternative or associated words: Unspecified verb (Bandler, 2008b: 320).

Bavister and Vickers (2004: 190) suggest that the following verbs could function in this capacity:

- experience;
- feel;
- understand;
- sense;
- learn.

EXAMPLE

- *'And you can make many changes.'*
- *'I want you to learn this.'*
- *'And what you know . . .'*
- *'And you can make sense of this.'*

The first and last examples, in particular, allow individuals to own and achieve or 'make sense of this' in their own way. This reduces resistance, particularly to change, and promotes an involvement approach.

3. Unclear noun (lack of referential index)

This is the same as the unspecified verb, but this time it is the noun that is not specified. The noun describes the person or object. Once again listeners have to search and determine the meaning of what has been said in order to understand it; their own interpretation potentially is more significant.

Alternative or associated words: Lack of referential index (Bandler, 2008b: 320).

The following are examples of this language pattern:

- 'A person might consider . . .'
- 'He broke it.'
- 'And they are not a part of me any more.'
- 'They can change more quickly than you think.'
- 'There are things that are important around you.'
- 'People can change.'

Generalisations

1. All of the same (universal quantifiers)

This pattern is used to generalise the listener's experience and is useful. It is described by Wake (2010: 121) as 'a set of words having universal generalisations or no referential index'.

Alternative or associated words: Universal quantifier (Bandler, 2008b: 318).

In order for us to learn to do things we tend to generalise to avoid relearning. According to Boyes (2006: 109) generalisations allow individuals to expand their thinking and 'open out to new ideas'. She refers to a universe with 'no reference points' and provides the following example: 'And everything that you experience as you listen allows you to understand deeply' (2006: 109).

The following words are examples:

- all;
- every;
- never;
- ever;
- always;
- nobody;
- no one;
- each;
- many;
- any.

The following sentences are also examples of how universal quantifiers can be used:

- 'And every time you stop you notice how much more . . .'
- 'And all the positive learning you've experienced . . .'
- 'There are many approaches you can take.'
- 'No one can ever fail once they decide to change.'
- 'Just think of all the ways this can be helpful to you.'

2. Mood controllers (modal operators)

Here the speaker will use words to focus the listener's experience in a certain direction. These words imply possibility or necessity and can be used to suggest rules. They are very useful for bypassing resistance, because they point out what it is possible to notice and not what the listener should be or is not noticing. No one can really argue with the possibility of things (O'Connor and Seymour, 2002).

EXAMPLE

'An individual could . . .'

'Could' in this instance can be followed by 'achieve great things' or 'be the very best they can be'.

People will automatically relate to themselves when thinking about 'An individual can . . .' Replacing 'can' with 'might' will also have the same effect of creating possibility.

Once an individual's mood controller word is identified, for example 'I need to', this word can be used to motivate the person to complete a given task. It can be effectively used both in emails and verbally.

The following are examples:

- might;
- should;
- can;
- could;
- will.

- 'Have you noticed that you can do this?'
- 'As you notice that you will learn a little bit every day . . .'
- 'And I wonder if you might start this behaviour right away or . . .'
- 'That you may feel . . .'
- 'That you could learn . . .'
- 'That you can change . . .'

Boyes (2006: 109) suggests that 'a modal operator of necessity allows the listener to form new rules of behaviour for himself' and provides the following example: 'You should take this opportunity to change . . .'

ACTIVITY **9.3**

Using mood controllers

- *Write three sentences using the mood controllers to imply something different for the listener to consider.*
- *Write three sentences using the mood controllers to suggest why someone should consider working with you.*

Additional Milton model language patterns

1. Linkage language

This is a word or grammatical component such as 'and' or 'because' expressing a cause or 'transition' (Churches and Terry, 2010: 54). Here the speaker will link or connect between suggestions and statements of fact, starting with something that is already occurring and linking it to something that he or she wants the listener to connect to.

In writing, the expectation is that ideally there should be one idea in each paragraph. Nevertheless, with the enunciated word the grammatical guidelines do not apply. The conscious mind will notice grammatical errors. The unconscious mind takes much more information in. Linkage words allow strings of ideas to be put together within a continuous sentence. The conscious mind is unable to keep track, leaving the unconscious mind to absorb all the information.

There are three types of linkage, and they vary in strength:

1. The weakest connection makes use of conjunctions to link items that would normally not be at all related. For example: 'You are sitting here relaxing, and you notice how you are beginning to drift' or 'Your breathing is slow and rhythmic, and you are getting curious about what you are going to feel next.'
2. The second uses linkage words such as 'like', 'as', 'while', 'during', 'when', 'since', 'soon' and 'such as', and they connect the unrelated items by establishing a link to time. For example: 'As you are relaxing more and more deeply you feel yourself drifting away', 'While you listen to my voice, can you notice which hand feels heavier?' or 'During this relaxation, I wonder if you are aware how much more . . .?'
3. The third is the strongest kind, as it uses words that actually state the causality, such as 'requires', 'causes', 'forces' and 'makes'. For example: 'The smooth running of the meeting will make the decision easier to reach.'

2. Presuppositions

The Milton model offers some other language patterns that are very useful and are present in the majority of sentences. The most important and powerful is the use of presuppositions. Hall (2001: 127) describes a presupposition 'as ideas and beliefs that we assume from the beginning as true and real'. He also reports that, in language patterns, presuppositions contain the working and hidden assumptions that drive an individual's interpretation of the world; they are the hidden meanings in sentences and can be used in an indirect way. An example of applying a presupposition would be to provide an individual with a number of choices; however, all the choices lead to a presupposed or wanted response.

The key to using presuppositions according to Wake (2010: 131) 'is to place them within a sentence so that the individual has to accept the presuppositions to make sense of the sentence'. For example: 'As you understand this so quickly, we can move on with some examples.' In this sentence, the speaker presupposes everything after 'as' and therefore that the listener has quickly understood everything and can move on and promptly learn more.

Putting adverbs before verbs and adjectives before nouns ensures that what follows is presupposed and potentially accepted as true.

Presuppositions can be challenged if they are limiting an individual's thinking, as discussed in Section 8, by using advanced questioning (the meta-model). However, in the Milton model they are applied to encourage individuals to think beyond their limiting beliefs and as a consequence create greater choice. Despite there being many presuppositions we tend to use seven, which are outlined below.

1. Time as a focus

The following are examples of the words identified in this group. They start a sentence or clause: 'before', 'after', 'begin', 'while', 'during', 'since', 'as', 'prior', 'when', 'was', 'current', 'later', 'early', 'earliest', 'latest', 'continuously' and 'eventually'.

Alternative words or classification: Subordinate clause of time (Bandler and La Valle, 2002: 35).

These are very useful for presentations, emails and letters to reduce resistance. For example:

- 'Before I start to explain, I want you to consider a few things.'
- 'After you finish your report, start working on the project.'

- 'As you learn how to use these language patterns you begin to notice how powerful they are.'
- 'Eventually you will see the benefits of your hard work.'

2. Number order

These words assume action will be taken and denote the order, for example 'another', 'first', 'second' and 'third'. They indicate the numeric sequence or a list (Wake, 2010).

Alternative words or classification: Ordinal presuppositions (Bandler, 2008b: 318).

The following are examples of the use of numbers in sentences as persuasive language:

- 'First, I want you to listen carefully to the language I am using and, second, think about how best these language patterns can be used in your work.'
- 'First, listen; second, take notes; and third, transcribe them into a document.'
- 'Do you want to take questions now or settle down into your presentation first?'

These examples can be used in written communication to create flow and acceptance of the ideas proposed.

3. Use of 'or'

This example of persuasive language refers to the use of 'or' between given choices. Wake (2010: 130) suggests that 'or' is the basis of a 'double bind', which is created by providing a choice but the extent of the choice is predetermined. For example:

- 'I am not sure if this is a pattern that you will find useful all the time or some of the time.'
- 'Should I see you today or tomorrow?'
- 'I wonder if you will start to notice how much more persuasive you are becoming straight away or within a few days.'
- 'Do you want to meet this Wednesday or next Thursday?'

The use of 'or' verbally can create the illusion that choice is being provided, and the individual will naturally pick one of the two, or reconcile the statement made to be true. This creates an agreement and assumes an action will follow.

4. Awareness predicates

Once more, these words are used to ensure that everything that follows is presupposed to be true. They suggest insight and perception. 'Know', 'aware', 'realise' and 'notice' are examples of awareness predicates. For example:

- 'I know that you will notice how useful this is as you become aware of this language pattern's power.'
- 'I wonder if you realise how knowledgeable you are.'
- 'Start to notice how positive this is.'
- 'By just noticing, your awareness will increase.'
- 'You may already realise how you are becoming more aware of self.'

More examples include 'grasp', 'discover', 'consider', 'experience', 'sense', 'understand', 'conceive' and 'perceive'. Again, used verbally these words create the suggestion of knowing and flow.

5. Adverbs and adjectives

Conversationally and in written communication these create flow and little resistance. These words can also presuppose that something is going to happen.

'Deeply', 'easily' and 'curious' are examples of adverbs and adjectives.

- 'I am curious about how easily this starts to come to you as you begin to use it more and more.'

More examples include 'readily', 'usually', 'finally', 'instinctively', 'truly', 'steadily' and 'naturally'.

6. Change of time verbs and adverbs

These verbs and verb tenses move the individual through time; for example, words ending in 'ing' suggest that something is 'ongoing', whereas the ending 'ed' denotes the past (Wake, 2010: 130).

Changing time in a sentence to the past as though something *had* happened can help someone currently 'stuck' in the present with a problem see the possibility of it being overcome. 'I am having problems with my boss' becomes 'I had a problem with my boss.'

The following also act as cue words: 'begin', 'end', 'stop', 'start', 'now', 'continue', 'proceed', 'already', 'yet', 'still' and 'any more'. For example:

- In the beginning you might have to think about it; as you continue it gets easier, and, as you realise that you already use it, it will become easier still.
- Steven decided to end the meeting and stop the deliberating now.
- You can continue to understand. (This presupposes that you understand already.)

7. Commentary adjectives and adverbs

These linkage words create no resistance and improve the flow. They connect sentences easily. Commentary adjectives and adverbs include 'fortunately', 'luckily', 'innocently', 'happily', 'spontaneously', 'necessarily', 'pleasantly', 'surprisingly', 'automatically' and 'interestingly'. For example:

- 'Fortunately, this is really easy and, although you have used this, luckily it is very straight-forward.'

Used in emails, these words can reduce any tensions or, if there is a difficult message, can make it more palatable.

Combining everything (stacking presuppositions)

Using different presuppositions on top of each other (stacking) makes them very hard to track on the unconscious level, so they tend to be accepted. 'Stacking presuppositions' are 'particularly powerful' (Bandler and La Valle, 2002: 38). For example: 'Firstly, before we resolve all the items on the agenda, I want you to start thinking about the opportunities this project offers, secondly what we have learnt so far and thirdly any additional ideas to implement. As we start the meeting we will have the opportunity to hear your views, as I know you all have a lot to contribute. As we continue with the minutes of the meeting, resolutions will become obvious, leading to mutual conclusions. Fortunately we all want the same outcomes and will happily work together, committed to the partnership and the success of this project.' You will notice the above sentences simply flow.

87

ACTIVITY **9.4**

Using presuppositions

Write a job advert using all of the above presuppositions.

---

3. Subtle commands (embedded commands)

In this pattern there is a command or directive, but instead of it being obvious it is embedded within a sentence. When a message or directive is embedded it can be delivered and accepted with ease. The simplest way to compile an embedded command is first to identify the command and then construct the sentence around it.

The statement verbally is marked with a slight change in voice tone by altering the speed, pausing or increasing the depth, with the inflection in the voice down to denote a command. The unconscious likes what is similar and notices what is different. Changing the voice to mark the command will therefore make the statement distinct. The conscious, however, is not aware of the command and instead accepts the statement; there is therefore no resistance. This language pattern is also very useful when combined with ambiguities.

Alternative or associated word: Embedded command (Bandler, 2008b: 322).

EXAMPLE

Command: *'Soon you will feel better.'*
Embedded: *'As you rest and look after yourself, soon you will feel better.'*

Command: *'Buy now our product.'*
Embedded: *'By now our product has helped many people on their journey of self-awareness.'*

Command: *'Trust me.'*
Embedded: *'I don't expect you to trust me until . . .'*

Bavister and Vickers (2004: 195) suggest putting a person's name after the mood or modal operator ('can', 'may', 'must'), which will individualise the command. For example: 'Everyone must, Amanda, listen carefully.'

ACTIVITY **9.5**

Embedded commands

Write three sentences using embedded commands. Start by identifying the command before inserting it into a sentence.

---

4. Command questions (embedded questions)

Questions that are commands can also be hidden within a sentence; because the command is embedded, the listener has no resistance as the conversation flows but instead responds internally as if the question was asked directly. There is no overt response required, and the individual accepts the information. The embedded question is marked with a change in voice tone, according to Boyes (2006: 114) 'as if you have an auditory highlighter pen'.

Alternative or associated word: Embedded question (Bandler, 2008b: 238).

Bavister and Vickers (2004: 195) suggest that the following words are useful: 'wonder', 'curious', 'know' and 'understand'. Asking a question with these words requires no response. For example:

- 'I am wondering what you would like to learn next.'
- 'I am curious to know how this will benefit you.'
- 'I am wondering when you will make the decision by.'
- 'I wonder which team member will notice your increase in self-esteem.'

ACTIVITY **9.6**

Embedded questions

Write down two things that you would want to elicit and then embed them in a longer sentence.

---

5. Negative or contradicting commands

Mentally, we do not have the ability to process a negative. Negation does not exist in sight, sound or feelings. If I said to you 'Don't think of pink elephants', you would first have to think of pink elephants to understand the statement and then decide how to do the 'don't'.

In much the same way, we give negative commands to our colleagues, teenagers, children, peers and so on without realising the power of negative commands. We tell young children 'Don't run' and they run faster. If you remove the negative – 'Don't' – what is left is the command that a person receives unconsciously and proceeds to follow.

In many organisations you will observe signs which say 'Don't' when in fact they should read 'Do', as this is the effect the command has. So, as the brain cannot process a negative, here we propose using this principle to provide a command, directive or suggestion.

Alternative or associated words: Negative commands (Bandler and La Valle, 2002: 39).

For example:

- 'Don't believe just in what I am saying.'
- 'Don't take my word.'
- 'Don't make any decision until you . . .'
- 'Don't let yourself forget . . .'

Negative commands

Think of a command that you want the listener to follow and then embed the negative instruction within it. Provide two examples.

6. Subtle form of asking (tag question)

This language pattern is helpful in getting specific responses from the listener indirectly. It is a very subtle form of asking, where the question is placed at the end of a statement, which creates a form of agreement as the individual concentrates on answering the question (tag). The so-called 'tag' therefore softens the statement, reducing any resistance (Wake, 2010). It has the structure of a question; however, the tonality used is that of a statement.

Alternative or associated word: Tag questions (Bandler, 2008b: 320).

For example:

- 'Don't you think?'
- 'Isn't it?'
- 'Couldn't you?'
- 'Aren't you?'
- 'Won't you?'
- 'Haven't you?'
- 'Can't you?'
- 'Will you?'
- 'Didn't you?'
- 'Weren't we?'
- 'Wouldn't you?'
- 'Aren't they?'

The following sentences contain a tag question:

- 'That was easy, wasn't it?'
- 'Do listen, will you?'
- 'You are becoming more aware, aren't you?'
- 'You think this is straightforward, don't you?'

Churches and Terry (2010: 52) describe the 'yes' tag of ending a sentence with, for example, 'wouldn't it?' and nodding at the same time to create a 'yes' response. This is particularly effective when used in a sentence with a number of facts followed by an embedded command and then the 'yes' tag, for example fact + fact + fact (embedded command) and then the 'yes' tag. For example: 'Today we decided to meet at 2 p.m. to plan the way forward. It is now 4.10 p.m. and we have 20 minutes left; now would be a good time to think creatively, wouldn't it?'

7. Conversational assumptions (conversational postulates)

Postulates simply ask, demand or claim. They are used as 'yes' or 'no' questions to request an action or ask for information. Because of the framing of the question, listeners are more compelled to complete the deed. The structure of the question allows listeners to feel as though they are able to choose to respond, without the question being authoritarian.

Alternative or associated words: Conversational postulates (Bandler, 2008b: 322).

This language pattern is used to avoid resistance, for it allows individuals to think they have a choice, but unconsciously it is received as a command. O'Connor (2001: 180) suggests it 'avoids giving a direct instruction' and instead appears to offer choice.

Think of what response you want from the listener, establish what has to be true (in other words, what can you presuppose?) and turn it into a question. When asking, you would use a deeper inflection in your voice, which denotes a command tone.

EXAMPLE

Outcome: *You want them to imagine having more confidence.*
Question: *'Is confidence something you can imagine having?'*

Outcome: *You want them to be able to do something specific.*
Question: *'Can you see yourself doing this?'*

Outcome: *You want them to arrive for a seminar at 9 a.m.*
Question: *'Are you able to arrive for 9 a.m.?'*

Outcome: *You want them to relax.*
Question: *'Can you relax now?'*

---

8. Double meaning (ambiguity)

This occurs when one word, phrase or sentence has more than one interpretation. When something has a double meaning it is known to be ambiguous, as it can be understood in more than one way. A form of mild confusion allows individuals to interpret and actively participate in making sense of the message which most probably will be more appropriate for them.

The following are examples of different forms of ambiguity.

1. Sound ambiguity (phonological ambiguity)

Phono is the Greek word for 'sound'; sound ambiguities are words that sound the same but have different meanings and spellings. These words can be marked out analogically and combined to create different meanings. These types of words are also known as homonyms.

Alternative or associated word: Phonological ambiguity (Bandler, 2008b: 324).

For example: 'there'/'their'; 'knows'/'nose'; 'knot'/'not'; 'here'/'hear'; 'I'/'eye'; 'bare'/'bear'; 'night'/'knight'; 'weight'/'wait'; 'bye'/'buy'/'by'; 'write'/'right'/'rite'.

They can also be used in combination with embedded commands. Churches and Terry (2010: 57) provide the following example: 'You know how to say no, and knowing that . . . you could begin to [embedded command].'

ACTIVITY *9.8*

Ambiguous words

Identify words that are ambiguous and then construct sentences with them.

2. Sentence ambiguity (syntactic ambiguity)

Sentence ambiguity refers to the formation of the sentence in the grammatical sense; the ambiguity is that the listener cannot determine the function of the word from the context that it is used in.

Alternative or associated words: Syntactic ambiguity (Bandler, 2008b: 324).

For example:

- 'They are visiting relatives.' (It is unclear whether they are the ones who are visiting or the relatives are visiting.)
- 'Flying planes are dangerous.' (Is it the act of flying planes that is dangerous, or is it planes that fly that are dangerous?)
- 'They were changing strategies.' (Were people changing the strategies, or were the strategies changing?)
- 'They are training teachers.' (Are they training people to become teachers, or are the people teachers who are doing training?)
- 'I am glad that I am a student and so is Lucy.' (Are Lucy and I glad that I am a student, or are Lucy and I glad that we are both students?)

The way to create syntactic ambiguity is to take a verb, add 'ing' and place it before the noun. Syntactic ambiguity can be used to introduce humour.

ACTIVITY *9.9*

Syntactic ambiguity

Write a sentence containing syntactic ambiguity.

3. Reference ambiguity (scope ambiguity)

The reference, or scope, means the extent or range of view. In other words, it is unclear how much of the sentence an adjective, word or phrase applies to: all or just one part of the sentence.

Alternative or associated word: Scope ambiguity (Bandler, 2008b: 324).

For example:

- 'We will go with the charming men and women.' (It is unclear if both the men and the women are charming, or just the men.)
- 'Relax as you feel the heaviness in your hands and your feet.' (Do you feel relaxed in both your hands and feet, or just hands?)
- 'Speaking to you as a man.' (Am I a man or are you?)

- 'Seeing you as a new student.' (Am I seeing you as a new student, or am I seeing you now that I am a new student?)

ACTIVITY **9.10**

Scope ambiguity

Write out three sentences containing scope ambiguities.

---

9. Patterns in metaphor

'The essence of metaphor is understanding and experiencing one kind of thing in terms of another' (Lakoff and Johnson, 1999: 5). Sullivan and Rees (2009) suggest that metaphor is crucial to the 'process of thinking'. It involves comparing one thing to another and can be used to concentrate information, making it easier to work with. Metaphors can also epitomise experiences more completely than 'abstract concepts', producing better communication and deeper and more profound thinking and learning. Because metaphors don't sound real to the listener there is no resistance to hearing the message. However, in order to understand the metaphorical message, we need to make an internal representation of the message; as the brain is unable to distinguish between fantasy and reality it will accept the message as real. Metaphors can be made up of similes, parables, anecdotes, analogies and literary metaphors.

Sullivan and Rees (2009) propose that human beings have an innate propensity to think and communicate in metaphor, with storytelling an integral part of human evolution. They suggest that individuals are 'hardwired to respond to metaphor and often do so unconsciously'. Lewis, Passmore and Cantore (2009) argue that all we convey is in a story format and that 'an account' of an occurrence cannot ever be exactly what happened; it is the perspective of an experience translated into words, with the predictability of something being misplaced or gained in the process.

In addition, the use of a particular metaphor can say more about individuals' thinking than their actual words and sentences. Indeed, Lawley and Tompkins (2000) suggest that we have personal metaphors, evidenced by the individual phrases and expressions used. The metaphors provide clues as to what is important, to experiences and to how we have assimilated, adapted or otherwise.

Simple metaphors according to O'Connor and Seymour (2002: 121) would include 'as white as a sheet' and 'as pretty as a picture'.

The following are often key indicators of a metaphor:

- It's like . . .
- It's as if . . .
- It's as though . . .

Examples of metaphor include:

- 'The next step.'
- 'Give me a hand.'
- 'Things are looking up.'
- 'Dealing with him is like being on a rollercoaster, except that on a rollercoaster you know it's going to end soon.'

(Sullivan and Rees, 2009: 26)

Metaphorical stories

Here we give qualities to something or someone that could not possibly have them. Listeners have to find a way for this to make sense, so they will probably apply the statements to themselves. This process is not a conscious one, but an automatic way of understanding what is going on (Sullivan and Rees, 2009).

The right brain is stimulated by a metaphor, and individuals are able to elicit from the story whatever is the most pertinent and fitting for their map of reality. A metaphor is not confrontational in the same way that a direct statement can be. The process is about reflection, interpretation and in the analysis learning.

Fairy tales, film, theatre and TV programmes are all examples of metaphors. Individuals will identify with a character, the hero or the heroine and compare the unfolding story to personal references and experiences. This pattern matching and recognition process is a natural survival instinct and is a rapid unconscious sequencing. Tapping into this natural instinctive learning process is uniquely powerful.

Stories also provide the medium for important lessons, culture, collective values, wisdom and knowledge within communities to be shared and passed on to different generations. The following is an example of a silly story; however, there are discernible messages to see and reflect on: 'Once upon a time there was a very accomplished red hat. Now all the wise old books did not really feel that the hat had reason to feel so accomplished. The wise old books thought that one needed more time and more experience in order to become accomplished . . .' For this story to make sense, listeners would have to apply it to themselves and, in doing so, take on board the lessons provided. The more the story echoes with our 'lived experience', the more likely it is to resonate (Lewis, Passmore and Cantore, 2009).

Stories can:

- relax individuals and put them at ease;
- provide an alternative perspective without appearing to preach;
- create possibilities beyond the usual thinking patterns;
- tap into the potential for lateral thinking and solving problems;
- encourage someone who is procrastinating to make a decision and act;
- identify risks or potential risks;
- reduce conflict;
- establish and increase rapport;
- improve team building;
- convince individuals about an idea;
- be used as part of a performance review;
- increase a negotiation opportunity;
- create deep critical reflection;
- be used to discuss change and transitions;
- challenge behaviour;
- summarise;
- achieve a compelling presentation.

You may think that you have no stories to tell. However, if you stop for a moment and reflect, you will see that everything we do is like a story (our subjective map of reality), our own 'soap opera'. This perspective changes our repertoire and flexibility to use these instinctive strategies.

Metaphors and metaphorical stories are powerful, persuasive and influencing language patterns. They create opportunities to communicate with impact.

How to use metaphor

- Practise listing your stories and reflecting on good stories you can use from everyday experiences.
- Raise your awareness to comments being made; for example, 'It's an uphill struggle' can hint that someone may be feeling overwhelmed. Simply asking how that feels can open up the reality, providing an opportunity to share a 'story'.
- Asking someone to describe a problem as a metaphor can help create enough detachment to gain a different and greater perspective. Both these examples can be simple conversation opportunities.
- When using a story as a metaphor, decide what is appropriate, matched to the audience. Too close a match and the metaphor's impact will be limited. Create the story with aspects of the current issue(s), including a sense of where 'the desired' is and a way forward to move from one to the other. Include representations of the 'real world' as characters within the metaphorical presentation, with a defined beginning, middle and end. Use all the language representational systems for a group, and individualise with smaller numbers. Embedded suggestions can be used, together with all the positive non-verbal reinforcements and expressions. 'Stacking presuppositions' will help the story to flow. Be attentive and 'tuned in' throughout, and create pauses of suspense and anticipation with your breathing.

What the research says

Cheal (2008), in his examination of the role of NLP in managing organisational paradox, suggested that the use of metaphor has a promising place in identifying and challenging paradoxical thinking. Examples of either/or, win/lose scenarios, group think indecision, conflicts, competing demands and mixed messages were cited as some examples of paradox. Listening for metaphors as expressions and clues and providing solutions in the form of metaphor were proposed (Cheal, 2008).

10. Selectional restriction violation

A selectional restriction violation refers to an inanimate object being given the qualities of an animate being, for example 'intelligence' or 'feelings' (Bandler, 2008b: 323). For example:

- 'Your outcomes want other people to change, not you.'
- 'The wise old books.'
- 'The accomplished car.'

ACTIVITY **9.11**

Storytelling

Working in a group, each individual identifies one inanimate object, for example a table, and an emotion, for example excitement. One person starts telling the story using the inanimate object and the emotion, for example the excited table. The next person introduces his or her object, and this continues until everyone has spoken. The story should refer to learning and accomplishment and contain an element of motivation and tenacity.

---

11. Quotes

Often, when a speaker delivers a message, it is not well received by the listener. However, if the message is from a third party, it is more likely to be accepted and considered (O'Connor, 2001). Milton Erickson used to do this all the time, making reference to his friend 'John'.

This format provides figurative distance between the issue and a third-party perspective. It is received in much the same way as a metaphor, the unconscious matching the pattern and interpretation to 'self'. It conveys the sense that someone else has solved a problem or approached a similar issue and there was a resolution.

Quotes can also provide an authority or expert perspective which is extremely credible. In a field where an evidence base is an important feature, using research and expert opinions can be compelling. For example: 'One of my brother's colleagues used to cycle for one week every two months.' More than likely if you told someone to do this, the person would refuse. However, in this format, he or she might entertain the idea: 'What one of my friends did was ask her neighbours to walk her dog for her.' Again, if you tell someone to do this, the person will most likely resist. However, as a third-party quote, it is more likely to be entertained.

ACTIVITY 9.12

Quotes

Working in a group, each person presents a problem and identifies a quote to resolve the issue. Notice if you feel that it is all right for you to do what is being suggested.

---

12. Other words to consider

1. 'Because' pattern

The word 'because' is very influential; it can be inserted in a sentence followed by almost any reason and it will be accepted with a 'yes' response. This works because the brain is conditioned, as part of the evolution process, to look for reasons, and is therefore more likely to accept anything after the word 'because'. For example: 'This is easy to follow because it is written down.' The 'because' strategy creates the motivation in a sentence of acceptance.

2. 'The more, the more'

Using the double comparison decreases resistance and increases acceptance of ideas, suggestions or actions. For example: 'The more you consider the proposition, the more you will realise the benefits.'

3. Agreement framework

Using 'I understand' can create resistance, and a possible response might be 'How could you possibly understand?' or 'How could you? You don't understand.' And this is true, for one individual cannot possibly have experienced exactly the same thing as another. Even if every detail is the same, the people are different, following their own versions of the 'map of reality'. A better response would be to use any of the three following suggestions:

- 'I appreciate . . .'
- 'I respect . . .'
- 'I agree . . .'

This is aptly called the 'agreement framework' (Howard, 2011: 4.14) and can be used whenever there is a particularly heated discussion or potentially difficult conversation. Other agreement frameworks are described elsewhere; discuss getting an individual to say 'yes' with respect to something inconsequential before seeking a 'yes' to something more significant and important.

Words to be used with caution

1. 'But flip'

The use of 'but' in a sentence negates or cancels out what has been said before it:

- 'I really want this but . . .'
- 'I am very pleased with the project work to date but not with your attendance.'

To reverse the impact (flip), respond with one of these:

- 'So you are not pleased with my attendance but you are very pleased with my project work.'
- 'I very much want my team to join the programme, but there isn't the time to release them.'

To delete the negativity, use: 'So there isn't the time to release the team to join the programme but you do want them to attend.' Alternatively, you can use 'and', 'because' or 'however' to substitute for 'but' if you do not wish to negate what is being stated. Adding the 'because' to the above examples makes the sentence even more powerful: 'So there isn't the time to release the team but you do want them to attend the programme because you know the value this will give your company.'

When people are unsure or feeling pessimistic they use the cautionary phrase 'yes but', which can dismiss and negate the comments made. A common retort is another 'yes but', and with it the two people conversing move linguistically further apart. Using 'OK' as a 'but flip' instead in this instance may simply be enough to change the direction of the conversation.

2. 'Try'

When people say that they will 'try to . . .' there is a presupposition that they may fail. A very common saying is 'I will try to phone you.' And most people don't. Youell and Youell (2011: 99) suggest that it creates an embedded command that sets the 'expectation that you will not succeed' which is implicit for both the individual and the listener. They recommend instead enquiring: 'What would it take to just do it?' This focus will help individuals to reflect on what will help them to do it. The rhyme 'Try is a lie' is the simple way to remember why not to use this word.

3. 'Issue'

'It's a real issue' is a frequent phrase used within organisations to give permission not to succeed. The message it conveys is 'It's too hard', which colludes in maintaining the 'stuck' status quo. It closes the door to choice and opportunities and creates a cul-de-sac of despair.

Simply deciding to delete this word from your language and, when tempted to use it, substituting the rhyming word 'tissue' will noticeably banish it from your language repertoire and with it the prevailing influence of being stuck. 'It's a problem' has a similar effect on your thinking. When you think of the word 'problem' it creates unhelpful images and thought associations.

This is not to imply that there are no challenges in our daily lives or that they can be ignored by simply changing the words we choose. It is about how we use language to influence our thoughts positively and, quite simply, how what we are telling ourselves and others can, as

Jacobson (1996: 59) would state, spread 'thought viruses' or not. Choosing instead the words of possibility creates a different frame and associations and, with them, opportunities to be more creative.

We have all been in the company of people who should be given Oscars for moaning, and we can instantly recall that draining feeling. Some would say moaning is about 'getting it all off your chest'. An appropriate response would be: don't allow it to be there in the first place – change your words and with them the thought associations and feelings. Remember, it is what you're telling yourself moment by moment which influences how you feel, so *stop* if it's not working and change your words.

Being kind to 'self first' may be a foreign land. However, in Gandhi's words, 'Be the change you want to see in the world.' This will serve as a reminder that your language choice will influence how others feel when in your presence. A 'reciprocal chain' of transformation then becomes possible.

4. 'If'
The word 'if' creates a sense of hesitancy and lack of clarity. Churches and Terry (2010: 55) advise that this word should be used with caution, as it implies the 'possibility of choice', except of course if you want to provide a choice.

5. 'You'
Avoid using the word 'you' in written and oral exchanges, particularly if it is a sensitive area. The word 'you' can be perceived as accusatory, aggressive and lecturing. Even saying something as innocent as 'You could consider this' sounds somewhat instructive, particularly if the subject is delicate. And too many 'you' words within a paragraph is the equivalent of pointing your finger. Remove the 'you' words, or use the word 'I' instead if it is appropriate; it is far more sincere.

Table 9.1 Summary – Milton model persuasive language

Pattern	Description	Classification	Example
Distortion	Altering reality	Mind reading	I know that they could . . .
	Cause to my effect	Cause and effect	Because you are here it will work.
	Linking one to another	Complex equivalents	As you read each chapter you will feel more relaxed about moving forward.
	Verb to noun	Nominalisation	The decision has been made.
	Value statement	Lost performative	You must finish a conversation on a positive note.
Deletions	Basic	Simple	They can achieve it.
	Compared to what?	Comparative	Language patterns are easier.
	Unclear verb	Unspecified verbs	You can work with these techniques.

Table 9.1 Continued

Pattern	Description	Classification	Example
	Unclear pronoun	Lack of referential index	They should know . . .
Generalisations	All judged the same Mood controllers	Universal quantifiers Modal operators	Everyone knows that . . . You might want to consider how you achieved the results.

Additional Milton

Pattern	Description	Classification	Example
1. Linkage language	Linking sentences	Linkage	As, when, because, while, soon.
2. Presuppositions	Time as a focus	Subordinate clause of time	Before, after, begin, during, since, as, prior, when, was, current, later.
	Number order	Ordinal numbers	Another, first, second, third, lastly.
	Use of 'or'		'Should I see you today or tomorrow?'
	Awareness predicates		'Start to notice how positive this is.'
	Adverbs and adjectives		Deeply, easily, curious, readily, truly.
	Change of time verbs and adverbs		Begin, start, stop, yet, now, continue.
	Commentary adjectives and adverbs		Fortunately, luckily, necessarily, surprisingly, automatically, interestingly, automatically.
3. Subtle commands		Embedded commands	The more you concentrate, the more you will learn new things.
4. Command questions		Embedded questions	I wonder which team member will notice your increased confidence.
5. Negative commands	Don't		Don't forget the negative comments.
6. Tag questions			And you can easily write this, can't you?
7. Conversational assumptions		Conversational assumption	Can you tell me which way?
8. Double meaning (ambiguity)	Sound ambiguity	Phonological ambiguity	You like me appreciate that this works.

Table 9.1 Continued

Additional Milton

	Sentence ambiguity	Syntactic ambiguity	They were changing approaches.
	Reference ambiguity	Scope ambiguity	Their deep understanding and rationale.
9. Patterns in metaphor			
10. Selectional restriction violations			The report eats him for breakfast.
11. Quotes			He said: 'Now is the perfect time.'
12. Other words	'Because,' 'The more, the more', 'But flip', 'Try', 'Issue', 'If', 'You'	Agreement framework	Because I am late can you let me go? The more you practise the more you will achieve. I like the sentiment but don't like the words. So you don't like the words but you like the sentiment. I will try to complete next week. Why do you want to do that? What stops you from writing it? If you stay for longer, you will relax.

TIPS FOR SUCCESS

- *Artful language strategies will provide you with powerful communication tools to influence change positively and help you work through any transitions.*
- *Adapt language patterns to match the competing demands, conflicting situations and myriad of complex scenarios you work in to secure effective and sustained relationships.*
- *Discover your unique and personal leadership style through the use of metaphors.*
- *Negotiate with the language of persuasion and influence. This will help you to achieve success.*
- *Create compelling speeches that motivate and engage individuals, and add these to your repertoire of leadership language tools.*

Section 10
Motivational language

Some people refer to the 'big picture'; others prefer to know the detail. External feedback and validation motivate some people, while others simply know inside that they've done a good job. These differences are referred to in neurolinguistic programming terms as the 'meta-programmes'; 'personal patterns' and 'thinking strategies' are Alder's (1996: 98) explanation. Bodenhamer and Hall (1997: 1) describe them as a wide range of deep unconscious 'frames of mind' from which an individual's attitudes and behaviours are governed. They are inextricably linked to values and are context specific, which means they can change across situations and that an individual's response may differ depending on whether he or she is at work or home (Wake, 2010).

From childhood we develop our patterns of behaviour, which become the meta-programmes, the filters which help us to make sense of, short-cut and categorise experiences. We established in Section 8 that this process of generalising is intrinsic and, while useful for learning, can create habitual 'blind spots'.

According to Rose Charvet (1997), Leslie Cameron-Bandler identified around 60 different patterns or 'meta-programmes'. These are defined by Rose Charvet as:

the specific filters we use to interact with the world. They edit and shape what we allow to come in from the outside world. They also mould what comes from inside ourselves as we communicate and behave in the world.

(1997: 11)

Bodenhamer and Hall (1997: 4) would add that the 'meta' represents the 'rules' we use to follow and make sense of or sort 'our thoughts and feelings'. Rose Charvet (1997) describes how Leslie Cameron-Bandler based this work on Chomsky's model of 'deletion, distortion and generalisation'.

Advantages of knowing about the meta-programmes

Knowing how individuals filter information by what they say is very effective, particularly when matching these internal processes to help motivate and create better rapport with people. Identifying a person's propensity for a particular programme or 'frame' is extremely powerful, together with understanding our own motivations and how they may affect others.

Meta-programmes are also useful when you pay attention to how people answer, as well as what they say. You will clearly be able to see what motivates one person and demotivates another by the language pattern that supports the behaviour. It can reveal what will make individuals do something and/or prevent them from acting in a certain way.

This enables you to know how to communicate more effectively and what to say specifically to capture and inspire. You will understand better what roles and tasks are suited to certain profiles. Mismatches between individuals' preferred styles and their professional roles can result in demotivation, with the side effect of poor performance. This knowledge of these linguistic patterns, however, will help you to work with, rather than become frustrated at, an individual who simply has a different style or preference.

According to Bavister and Vickers (2004: 51), 'most meta-programs come in pairs of bipolar opposites'. Individuals, however, do not fall absolutely into either/or categories but can be somewhere upon a spectrum. Furthermore, some of the programmes are in sets of three or four.

The following examples and explanations are based on Rose Charvet's (1997, 2010) work.

Proactive versus reactive (action)

The first group is about proactive versus reactive (see Table 10.1).

Questions to elicit whether an individual is reactive or proactive include:

- 'How would you go ahead and act on it?'
- 'How do you know when to start a task?'

According to Rose Charvet (1997: 24), 15–20 per cent of people are proactive and equally 15–20 per cent are reactive, with 60–70 per cent equally proactive and reactive. Use 'considering and doing' to meet both preferences.

Table 10.1 Proactive versus reactive (action)

PROACTIVE	
Typically	Proactive individuals take a lead, initiate, get involved, make decisions quickly, jump in, are action oriented and get things done. They assume leadership roles. They don't need much time to investigate or require motivating, for action and initiating are what influence these individuals. At the extremes they will act 'with little or no thinking', avoiding analysis and planning.
What they say	They use positive and present words. They speak as if they are directing everything/the world. They use short, snappy and clear statements. They maintain focused eye contact. They can be blunt. At an extreme they may 'bulldoze'. They speak fast, passionately and engagingly. They can be fidgety and animated. They may show signs of impatience. 'I have decided', 'Let's go for it', 'Why wait?' and 'We don't need to think about it' are statements they might make.

Table 10.1 Continued

PROACTIVE	
What you should say	'Go for it'; 'Jump in'; 'Just do it'; 'Why wait?'; 'Right away'; 'Get it done'; 'Run away with it'; 'Right now'; 'Let's do it now'; 'I'll make it happen'; 'Let's go for it'; 'I'll do it right now'; 'Time to act'; 'No one needs to sit around waiting'; 'Take control'; 'Don't wait.'

REACTIVE	
Typically	Reactive individuals need time to investigate a situation and the information to get a good understanding before being prepared to make a decision. They believe in 'chance and luck'. People can get frustrated with the lack of a 'self-starter' style. They wait for others to initiate and then respond; they may not take any action. They take time to think about things.
What they say	They use long or incomplete sentences, failing to get to the point. They use passive or inactive verbs, and nominalisations are common. They maintain little or no eye contact. They require extensive initiative. They talk about what they are thinking, understanding and considering. They use careful language and long statements. They use the words 'but', 'should', 'would', 'could', 'might' and 'may'. They typically say 'A decision has been made', 'Let's wait to find out more first' or 'Before we go any further I need to review all the details.'
What you should say	'Think about it'; 'Consider'; 'Wait'; 'Might'; 'Now that you have analysed this'; 'You'll get to really understand'; 'This will tell you why'; 'You might want to consider'; 'When the time is right'; 'When you think this through'; 'It's best to understand what will happen'; 'See what the others think'; 'After thoroughly understanding the issues'; 'Take your time.'

Toward versus away from (direction sort)

This second group is about motivation in relation to direction, with the bipolar concepts of moving towards and moving away from (see Table 10.2).

Questions to elicit whether an individual is toward or away from include:

- 'Why did you leave your last job?'
- 'What do you ultimately want?'
- 'What will having . . . do for you?'
- 'Why is having that . . . important?'

According to Rose Charvet (1997: 34), in the work context 40 per cent of the population are toward and 40 per cent away from, with 20 per cent equally toward and away from.

Table 10.2 Toward versus away from (direction sort)

TOWARD (PLEASURE)

Typically	'Pleasure' people are focused on wanting something or wanting outcomes. They think in terms of their future goals and what there is to accomplish, attain, gain, have, get or obtain, or the positive benefits. They ultimately move towards pleasure and rewards. Because they focus on their goals or outcomes so much they can make accomplished project managers. However, they may experience difficulties identifying problems or pitfalls and risks and are demotivated by a lack of clear goals.
What they say	They talk about gain, what they could achieve or their goals. Their body language is facing towards something, and the head may be nodding. They are focused on what they desire, their dreams and what they want. They use statements like 'If I do . . . I will get . . .', 'I would achieve personal satisfaction and a promotion', 'I could buy a new house when this is finished' or 'All my personal aims will be realised as a result of . . .'
What you should say	'Attain'; 'Obtain'; 'Get'; 'Have'; 'Include'; 'Achieve'; 'Enable'; 'Here is what you could accomplish'; 'Here is what you want'; 'The benefits of this are . . .'; 'When you do this the positive results are . . .'; 'The goal here is to . . .'

AWAY FROM (PAIN)

Typically	'Pain' people notice what they should avoid and are motivated by steering clear of or away from problems and circumstances that can cause, or have caused, previous pain. They are motivated by goals which move them away from problems. They are spurred on by avoiding threats and are good at identifying potential risks. Deadlines, pressure and problems to resolve motivate these individuals to act; however, they may be distracted by fixing problems and identifying priorities. Safety, security and protection are what they look for in a job. Inspecting and quality control are good roles for these individuals.
What they say	They will talk about things to avoid, evade and exclude. They describe potential problems, risks and issues. They can jump to all the things that could go wrong and focus on problem solving. Typical statements: 'There are lots of issues with this proposal'; 'If I don't get out there and deliver, I won't be able to pay the bills'; 'If you take your time and talk to all the staff you will avoid a grievance.'
What you should say	'Won't have to'; 'Solve'; 'Overcome'; 'Prevent'; 'Avoid'; 'Fix'; 'Not have to deal with'; 'Get rid of'; 'Let's find out what is wrong with it'; 'There will be no problems'; 'Here's how you can avoid this problem'; 'If it's not solved it will only get worse'; 'Do you see any problems with this proposal?'; 'Why not fix it now rather than wait for it to deteriorate?'; 'You will never have to deal with this again'; 'Prevent these adverse results'; 'Steer clear of'.

External versus internal (standards)

The third group of meta-programmes relates to how we evaluate. One approach is from an internal set of standards or references; the other is from external feedback (see Table 10.3).

A question to ask to elicit this motivation type is:

- 'How would you know you have done a good job?'

According to Rose Charvet (1997: 50), in the work context 40 per cent of the population are 'internal', 40 per cent are 'external', and 20 per cent are equally 'internal' and 'external'.

Table 10.3 External versus internal (standards)

EXTERNAL (outside criticism or feedback)	
Typically	External people need other people's views, outside direction and feedback from external sources to know how they are doing. To perform well they need external feedback, evidence and validation. Without external direction they may find difficulty starting tasks and without external feedback may experience problems continuing with a project or activity. They will make a decision on evidence. They are motivated by someone else's thoughts, title, status, car and so on. For external people it is about getting their needs met. They can appear overreactive, as they hear mild suggestions as directions. External people do not have 'internal standards' for themselves but rather compare and measure from external references, events and circumstances. They also naturally tend to compare their work with that of others. They may lean forward, watching your response and facial expression for clues, and look for all sources of possible feedback. They are good at helping people and service type roles.
What they say	They will seek out feedback. External references will provide the information. Outside information is taken as an order or decision. They may refer to other people valuing something and list what is good. 'My clients are happy. My boss is happy. I met my quota.' 'I like to receive daily feedback to know I am doing a good job.' 'I value their opinion as to whether I am cutting it.'
What you should say	'You'll get good feedback'; 'It has been approved by . . .'; 'You will make quite an impact'; 'Here's what people are saying about this'; 'So-and-so thinks . . .'; 'I'd appreciate if you would . . .'; 'What I've noticed'; 'The approval you will get'; 'Statistics or the results show . . .'; 'Others will notice.'

INTERNAL (self-criticism or self-evaluation)	
Typically	Internal people have their own standards or frames of reference and use these to compare and evaluate a course of action or completed work. They may find it difficult to accept other people's views, as they often decide for themselves and validate their own performance. They can hear external directions simply as information.

Table 10.3 Continued

INTERNAL (self-criticism or self-evaluation)	
	If they receive negative feedback they tend to question it and potentially reject it out of hand. They may also question the judgement of the person giving the feedback. They can be difficult to manage and supervise, and set standards which are not explicit. They can appear quite independent and like fully to express their core values and make their own decisions. They can stay motivated without the need for feedback. They may ignore external facts, advice and evidence, choosing instead to use their intuition. At the extreme of the spectrum they may not care what other people think.
What they say	They evaluate their own performance. They resist being told what to do. Outside instruction is taken as information. They decide and tend to use 'I'. They may mention their gut feelings. 'I know when I have done a good job.' 'I have set standards.' 'I don't need any feedback, thank you.' 'I just know.'
What you should say	'Only you can decide'; 'You might want to consider'; 'It's up to you'; 'You will know what to do'; 'What do you think?'; 'I need your opinion'; 'I value your opinion'; 'You must make the decision'; 'Does this meet your expectations?'; 'May I make a suggestion?'

Same versus different (relationship sort)

The next group of meta-programmes relates to sorting. Individuals sort in respect to either what they can match as common (similar) or what they notice is different (dissimilar) (see Table 10.4). For example, one person may identify a familiar theme; another may identify the exception to the rule or norm.

With this spectrum, the 'same' and 'different' represent the opposite ends. In between is 'sameness with exception' and 'difference with exception'. The 'sameness with exception' people will be comfortable with change, providing it is gradual, and can tolerate changes every two years with a significant degree of change every seven years; this would include a role or job change. The 'differences with exception' people would stay in a role or job for one to three years. They would change their car and holiday destination quite frequently and like reorganising.

Questions to ask to elicit this motivation type include:

- 'How long have you been in the job?'
- 'Would you tell me about your career?'
- 'On average how long do you stay in a job for?'

According to Rose Charvet (1997: 78), in the work context sameness extremes account for 5 per cent of the population, 'sameness with exception' accounts for 65 per cent, 'difference'

Table 10.4 Same versus different (relationship sort)

SAME (matching)

Typically	'Same' people want things to stay the same and value security. They will change companies but stay in the same job. They will change restaurant but eat the same meal. They may follow the same routines every day. They don't like change and may refuse to adapt. When an organisation undergoes restructuring changes or service redesign they are the ones who resist the most.
What they say	They will compare with others how they are the same. They will spot things that are the same. They will talk about what they have in common. They will notice how things have not changed. 'Things are still the same. I am still doing the same job!' 'I like to see the same person.' 'We always go there.' 'We don't like new things.'
What you should say	'This is the same as . . .'; 'In common'; 'As you always do'; 'Life before'; 'As you already know'; 'Exactly as before'; 'The same quality service as always'; 'What this has in common with the previous report'; 'What you've been used to'; 'You use this in just the same way as you always have done'; 'It is identical'; 'This part is unchanged.'

DIFFERENT (mismatching)

Typically	'Different' people prefer change. They thrive on it, resisting static situations and the status quo. They seek jobs that lack routine and change their jobs as frequently as every 6–12 months. They will go to new restaurants and choose different food from the menu all the time. Change inspires them. They frequently reorganise things. They like variety and newness and spot difference. Talking about new developments and adventure inspires them. Emphasising how things are different also motivates them. They can be difficult to talk to, as they will search out difference even in the arguments they make, which may present as them arguing the opposite just for the sake of it. They will also identify all the 'yes buts'.
What they say	They are not good in relationships. They will spot what is different in a situation. They focus on the destination and ignore the journey. 'It is totally different. I now work out in the field.' 'I enjoy the change.' 'It's great not to know what will happen every day.'
What you should say	'New'; 'Totally different'; 'Unlike before'; 'Unique'; 'One of a kind'; 'Completely changed'; 'Shift'; 'A complete turnabout'; 'A new process'; 'Brand new'; 'Revolutionary'.

accounts for 20 per cent, and 'sameness with exception and difference' accounts for 10 per cent.

Specific versus general (chunking)

This next meta-programme group relates to the size (chunk) or amount of information we prefer to process, whether this is general (global, 'big picture') or specific (detailed) (see Table 10.5).

There is no specific question to ask. The conversation will demonstrate preference; for example, a specific individual would provide too much information or detail, and the general individual would provide very little information.

According to Rose Charvet (1997: 96) in the work context 15 per cent of the population are specific, with 60 per cent general and 25 per cent equally specific and general.

Table 10.5 Specific versus general (chunking)

SPECIFIC (exact)	
Typically	Exact people handle small pieces of information well. They like detail, specifics, exactness and precision and will use appropriate names. They take information in linearly and work step by step in a sequence; if the sequence is interrupted they will start again from the beginning. They don't make big pictures. They notice detail in a tree rather than the whole forest. They are described as 'inductive thinkers' (Bodenhamer and Hall, 1997: 56), who start with the details and then move upwards (chunk up). They like as much information as possible and are the individuals who write copious amounts of notes so they don't miss any details. They like the details broken down into specifics. They are good at identifying small errors; however, they can become bogged down in the details. According to Wake (2010: 167) this individual would be equivalent to the 'sensor' in Myers–Briggs terms.
What they say	They speak in sequence, step by step. They use lots of adverbs and adjectives in their speech. They use proper nouns for people, places and things. If they lose the sequence they have to start again. They like figures, statistics and percentages. 'First give me the details and I will see.' 'Yesterday at 7.45 a.m. the postman came to deliver this parcel. He also brought the mail, but this parcel was wrapped in a very unusual way, as it was a box that was cut in half and had a strange shape.'
What you should say	'Exactly'; 'Precisely'; 'Detailed'; 'To plan'; 'Specifically'; 'Here are the precise steps that we can follow'; 'In detail'; 'Step by step'; 'Can I give you all the specifics?'

Table 10.5 Continued

GENERAL	
Typically	General people work with the big picture (an overview) and like abstract concepts. Précis, summaries and keeping the details to a minimum are what motivate. They can generate many ideas without implementing any of them. They are able to see how the end result will look, as they can process the whole picture and are comfortable with random order. They are very global and can lack detail in their plans. For that reason, there may be no logical order or sequence in how things unfold.
	They are described as 'deductive thinkers' (Bodenhamer and Hall, 1997: 56), who start globally and move downwards (chunk down). They can make good strategists. However, they can be described as not in touch or as having their 'head in the clouds'. These individuals don't like to read instructions and may generalise and delete information. They like general principles and themes and can miss important details.
	According to Wake (2010: 167) this individual would be equivalent to the 'intuitor' in Myers–Briggs terms.
What they say	They may present things in a random order.
	They are good for overviews.
	'Give me an overview and I will decide.'
	They use simple, basic sentences, with not much detail.
	'The postman delivered a parcel with the mail.'
	'I have nothing more to say.'
	'Basically it is fine.'
What you should say	'The big picture'; 'Overview'; 'The main idea'; 'Essentially'; 'The important thing is'; 'In general'; 'Basically'; 'In summary'; 'In essence'; 'In brief'.

Options versus procedures (responding style)

The next group of meta-programmes concerns the way we handle directions and whether someone follows the rules and methods or bends them (see Table 10.6). This is easily discernible in everyday activities.

A question to ask to elicit this motivation type is:

- 'Why did you choose . . .?'

A procedural person will answer this as a 'how' question and will use modal operators of necessity. Ask any 'why' question and listen.

According to Rose Charvet (1997: 64), in the work context 40 per cent of the population are options people, with 40 per cent procedures people and 20 per cent equally options and procedures.

Table 10.6 Options versus procedures (responding style)

OPTIONS (possibility)	
Typically	Doing things in a different way is the motivation for individuals with this preference. They are adept at identifying different strategies and designing new procedures. They don't like following standard procedures and instead are more motivated by finding improvements or alternative ways to the procedure. Unlimited possibilities, innovation, ideas and creativity are compelling to the 'options' individual. Variety, choice and bending the rules are key, as are freedom and controlling one's own future. Thinking outside the box is the preferred operating system. The freedom to explore is important. With the right work these individuals are 'self-starters', so start-up and service development would be appealing, rather than maintenance roles, including design and any remit which requires creativity and ideas. Commitment can be a problem, as it reduces the individuals' options. Decisions can also be a problem, as the individuals invent more possibilities and options. Unfinished projects and procrastination when faced with too many ideas (which the individuals have created) can be the down side. 'Options' individuals are no good at following their own procedures, which they may have been responsible for creatively designing. Routine tasks are not for these individuals.
What they say	They listen for the language of possibility, rationales and choice. They talk about the many possibilities, opportunities and alternatives. They may mention thinking outside the box. 'We could do it this way.' 'It might be better if we think of all the alternative strategies.' 'I would be happy to test that. I can imagine all the possibilities.'
What you should say	'Can do'; 'Could do'; 'It's a great opportunity'; 'You can break the rules'; 'There are unlimited possibilities'; 'We will play it by ear'; 'Can you think of another way?'; 'What do you think?'; 'What are the alternatives here?'; 'There must be a solution'; 'That's one approach.'
PROCEDURES (necessity)	
Typically	Individuals with this preference follow the prescribed ways, completing tasks following identified and established procedures. They are natural completers and finishers. They get things done and believe there is a right way of completing something. Once they have mastered a procedure they can repeat it many times. They can be more preoccupied with how to do something correctly instead of understanding the reasons why. Procedures with a clear beginning and ending are preferred. Without a procedure to follow such individuals can feel uncomfortable. 'Procedures' individuals do not like too many choices and are motivated by the thought of completing and finishing a task in the correct way. They may find it difficult to design a new procedure if it is expected to be radically different. They are good with rule-based administration.

Table 10.6 Continued

PROCEDURES (necessity)	
What they say	'Must'; 'Have to'; 'Need to'; 'Got to'. They often answer a 'why' question with 'how to'. They like to explain the stages and identify the steps. You can see procedural people marking out time or steps with their hands.
What you should say	'Follow this and you can't go wrong'; 'This is the tried-and-tested way'; 'This is the right way'; 'Firstly . . . then secondly . . . and finally . . .'; 'This is a reliable way of completing that'; 'The evidence shows this is the right procedure'; 'The methodology is important'; 'This is the best way'; 'Talk me through step by step.'

Independence versus proximity versus co-operation

The final meta-programme described in this chapter is made up of three dimensions in relation to affiliation and working with others. The three categories include: independence, proximity and co-operation (see Table 10.7).

Questions to ask to elicit this motivation type include:

- 'Can you tell me about a work situation where you worked to your best?'
- 'What made it successful?'

According to Rose Charvet (1997: 122), in the work context 20 per cent of the population are 'independence' people, with 60 per cent 'proximity' and 20 per cent 'co-operation'.

Table 10.7 Independence versus proximity versus co-operation

INDEPENDENCE (self only)	
Typically	Independent people are comfortable with sole responsibility and working alone. Productivity reduces if other people are around. They don't like to be interrupted and prefer to work in their own space, ideally with a door tightly shut between them and the rest of the world. They can find rapport building and what they perceive to be small talk difficult. They know what they need to function in their role but may not be aware what others require, and so they find it difficult to explain what someone should do to succeed. They can fulfil management roles; however, they can forget to engage with and consult others and may end up doing most of the work themselves. Given the choice they wouldn't really want to manage other people. They usually have a high degree of self-control. They can appear self-absorbed. Reading body language and subtle communication cues can be difficult for these individuals. They don't like distractions.
What they say	They use the word 'I' rather than 'we'. They rarely talk about other individuals. They don't talk a lot and prefer their own company. They will avoid office gossip and talking at the coffee machine. They can be very focused on the task and so talk only about work and work tasks.

Table 10.7 Continued

INDEPENDENCE (self only)

What you should say	'Complete this on your own'; 'We will make sure you have no interruptions'; 'This project will be your project'; 'You will have sole responsibility'; 'You can simply get on with it'; 'You have permission to divert your phone while you are completing this project'; 'You will have all the time you need to succeed.'

PROXIMITY (with others, but in control)

Typically	These are people who like to work with and manage others. They prefer directing and supervising people. They know what they and others need to do to succeed, and they like a specified span of control. Working through and with people, in clearly defined roles, is the way to motivate these individuals. They don't like working alone or sharing management responsibility with others. Suited to project management roles, they will ensure all individuals are aware of their defined responsibilities, including the project managers.
What they say	They use a mixture of 'I' and 'we' words. They will be specific about what their role is. They will also be specific about what other people's roles are. 'We can do this; I will do this part and you will . . .' 'This is my area of responsibility.' 'This is how we can work together.'
What you should say	'You will be working with the team but you will clearly be in charge'; 'Take control of this group task'; 'You are the project lead'; 'You have the responsibility for the team'; 'You are the lead for X'; 'You will direct the team.'

CO-OPERATION (shared responsibility)

Typically	These individuals like to work with people and belong to a team. They are usually good communicators, as they enjoy being with and talking to other individuals. They can be adept at understanding other people's motivations. They like to co-facilitate and, if they manage, to share responsibility. They like working with people to generate ideas and be productive. Not good at working alone, they will seek out other people. They can get carried away in conversations and may find it difficult managing their peers.
What they say	They use 'we' in all conversations. They will notice and enquire if someone is not communicative. They use language to invite and involve others. They will be the individuals who arrange the work social events. They like to use words such as 'We are a family here.'
What you should say	'We can do this together'; 'All of us'; 'Together we can achieve'; 'This is a team effort'; 'We will all get credit for this'; 'You can work with the group'; 'This is a team task'; 'Can you generate ideas with the group?'; 'Can you jointly facilitate this work?'

What does having knowledge of the meta-programming mean for individual managers and leaders?

- The meta-programme provides an important insight into how people take in information from the external world and process it differently, and how this influences their emotions, behaviour and preferences.
- An understanding of this programme is very powerful in managing and interacting with others. It is particularly helpful in bringing about a resolution in the most intractable conflicts, increasing an appreciation between individuals.
- The self-awareness gained from understanding the different preferences within the programmes is also powerful in managing self and others.
- Recognising other people's thinking preferences ensures that these can be matched to increase rapport and to communicate more effectively. This can be manifested in many different ways, particularly when used in combination with the meta-model, from verbal one-to-one interactions to written formats of communication.
- The amount of rapport you have with someone is equivalent to the degree of influence, or otherwise, you have over the person and therefore can determine how successful the communication is.
- Influencing others using the meta-programme allows the matching of ideas, creating greater clarity, particularly when explaining, for example, policies and directives to individual clients and other staff. Anyone who is interviewing can use these skills, from the recruitment of staff, getting the right match for the job, and organisation, to interviewing clients, parents and carers, matching their personal and very individual information requirements.
- Knowledge of the meta-programme arguably creates greater flexibility, particularly in establishing rapport with people who have a very different perspective or outlook. This flexibility reduces the chances of getting fixed on one outcome or solution, with potentially detrimental effects.

Whereas the meta-programmes help us organise our thinking and approaches to external issues, filtering what we let in and out, the submodalities are concerned with the sensory elements of our internal representations.

Part 4
Leading self

Section 11

Understanding and enhancing thought processes

Submodalities

The concept of how words individuals use provide an insight into the way they are representing (or re-presenting) information internally was discussed in Section 5. These representational systems, or modalities, each have more explicit qualities or 'submodalities'. According to O'Connor (2001: 94) 'the submodalities are the building blocks of the representational systems and how we structure our experiences'. They distinguish the 'intensity of meaning'; for example, when recalling a happy event, the amount of pleasure is a result of 'the colour, size, brightness and distance of the visual image you hold in your mind's eye' (Bandler and MacDonald, 1988: 2).

Submodalities are essentially how the mind internally organises events. They provide the clues in language to describe and appreciate experiences and what they represent. Bandler and MacDonald (1988: 2) suggest that people will use 'predicates (verbs, adverbs and adjectives) specific to the representation system they are functioning in'. Phrases like 'I just can't see a way out of this situation' or 'I have a good feeling about this' would typically be heard. An individual is unable to recall a memory or an experience without it having a 'submodality structure' (O'Connor and Seymour, 2002: 43).

Submodalities are the finer distinctions (details) and characteristics within each representational system. For example, some visual (seeing) submodalities include whether something is black and white or colour, framed or panoramic, 2D or 3D, moving or still, focused or unfocused, foreground or background, and associated (part of the picture) or dissociated (seeing yourself in the picture). Other visual submodalities include the size, shape, brightness, distance and location.

Not many people realise that communication creates internal visual images and that words are like linguistic anchors. The hypothesis that language has an impact on visual imagery is supported by research, according to Bolstad (2002: 19). Furthermore, in language the depth of someone's internal representation can be heard by listening for the submodalities, which add a deeper meaning to what is being said. When individuals think of ideas and principles, distinct areas within the brain associated with the modalities become activated (Pecher, Zeelenberg and Barsalou, cited by Tosey and Mathison, 2009: 65).

The categories or submodalities for each main representational system (visual, auditory, kinaesthetic, olfactory and gustatory) are detailed in Activity 11.1. The auditory digital representation (internal dialogue or 'self-talk') would typically have the following submodalities: location of the words; self- or others oriented; current, past or future tense; loud or soft; different voice depending on the situation.

The visual, auditory and kinaesthetic representations and the equivalent submodalities are groupings which are more frequently discussed than the auditory digital representation outlined above. However, mental conversations and the associated self-talk can be a way that an individual processes an experience. In contrast, thinking of a smell memory will first trigger a visual image; for example, if you think of the smell of an onion, you will picture an onion. Visual is the dominant internal representation system. In addition, the 'more visual' an 'input' is, the more likely it will be 'recognised and recalled' (Medina, 2008: 233).

Bavister and Vickers (2004: 42) describe two further distinctions of submodalities, 'digital and analogue'. For example, 'digital' are either 'on or off' (there or not) – a mental image is 'moving or still'. With 'analogue submodalities', there are many different variables between polarities: essentially a continuum. For example, there can be countless diverse colours varying in different degrees and contrasts. For most, as the brilliance of the image is intensified the reaction is also increased. The majority of submodalities are 'analogue' and are present all of the time (Bavister and Vickers, 2004: 42). Tosey and Mathison (2009: 65) stress that an individual uniquely encodes experiences, and therefore these are 'not generalisable'. It cannot be assumed, for example, that, if one person experiences anxiety, all people feel anxiety in the same way. All individuals need to be assessed and calibrated in the moment to be able to elicit an appreciation of their unique process.

Submodalities and thoughts

Every thought is converted in this way using pictures, feelings, sounds, tastes and smells (visual, kinaesthetic, auditory, gustatory and olfactory). We learnt earlier how the brain stores beliefs, experiences and values in the same way as it does for emotions using these five representational systems. Submodalities form the details which encode experiences of 'reality, certainty and time' (O'Connor, 2001: 94). Similar feelings create similar submodalities, for example happiness and pleasure, certainty and motivation. Anticipated future events and how someone feels currently also create submodalities and not just memories and past events.

O'Connor (2001: 95) suggests that all the submodalities have the same qualities in terms of the following:

Location	'All sense experience is experienced as coming from somewhere.'
Distance intensity	'The location will be a certain distance away – near or far.'
	'All sense experiences are measured as more or less intense.'
Associated or dissociated	'The individual will either be "inside" or "outside" the experience.'

According to O'Connor (2001: 95), the 'finer the discriminations we can make in our submodalities, the more clearly and creatively we can think'. He also suggests that eliciting people's submodalities is important in changing limiting or disempowering beliefs.

Changing perceptions using submodalities

Bavister and Vickers (2004) discuss how varying the submodalities can be very effective and potent and, importantly, can change the meaning of an experience and how a person responds to it. The emotional attachment can, therefore, be transformed. It should be remembered that changing the submodalities is not about altering what happened (the content); the event occurred and cannot be changed, but the way the brain encodes the sensed experience *can* be changed.

'The impact and meaning of a memory' are influenced more by the submodalities used to encode it than the original content (Bavister and Vickers, 2004: 43). McDermott and Jago (2003: 81) suggest that some submodalities are more 'critical' than others in terms of influencing and bringing about a change. They are described by Molden (2001: 69) as 'driver' or key submodalities, as they are stronger, and their effect is more powerful, as they act like 'master switches' of a representation. A bigger shift can be created by changing one of these key or 'driver' submodalities (Molden, 2001: 69). For example, if changing the size and location of an experience causes the most significant 'shift' then size and location are the drivers. In other experiences, if changing the auditory submodality will create the shift, auditory is the driver. This criticality is unique to each individual and the experience. Bolstad (2002) asserts that there is research which confirms that remembered and constructed images use identical neurones.

The submodalities can be changed to transform the effect they have and therefore the behaviours they can create. Individuals, for example, may have memories which can have an adverse impact on their present ability to cope with events, creating fear and low self-esteem. Other memories may generate pleasant feelings, which can be intensified and elicited when required to create a positive emotional state, for example before a presentation or meeting. It is also possible to attach the right positive submodalities to a goal so as to ensure its attainment is more attractive and therefore much more likely (Bavister and Vickers, 2004).

Submodalities are also 'systemic in that they tend to affect one another' (Bandler and MacDonald, 1988: 26). When the submodalities are changed by, for example, reducing a panoramic, colourful picture, which could be a representation of a bad memory (with associated anxious feelings), through encouraging the individual to visualise reducing its size, draining the colour or turning it to black and white, it can change the feelings attached to the original image and memory. Size and colour are two of the easiest submodalities that can be changed.

If there is an associated sound submodality with an image, this too can be adjusted to reduce or intensify the impact by changing or altering the volume, tone or direction of the sound. Kinaesthetic (feeling) submodalities after finding the location of the feeling can be changed by varying the movement and direction of the feeling.

Alder and Heather (1998: 109) remind us that individuals can adjust the way they 'represent or interpret the world' by simply changing their 'thought submodalities'. Activity 11.1 introduces how to elicit different submodalities as the beginning part of changing or shifting submodalities.

ACTIVITY **11.1**

Submodality comparisons

Elicit the submodalities of a positive and then a negative experience and detail these in the blank columns in Table 11.1. This is a useful exercise to complete with someone else. Notice the differences between the two experiences.

Some people, when asked to think of a memory or future event, can see clear pictures; for others, the image may be just a colour or shape or might be indistinct. The image can also be

Table 11.1 Submodalities comparison

Seeing (visual)	Experience 1 (positive)	Experience 2 (negative)
Number of images		
Moving/still (speed fast/slow)		
Colour/black and white		
Bright/dim/faded		
Focused/unfocused		
Bordered/panoramic		
Associated/dissociated		
Size		
Shape		
Three-dimensional/flat		
Close/distant		
Location in space		
Orientation		
Density		
Hearing (auditory)		
Number of sounds		
Type of sound, for example music		
Volume		
Soft/harsh		
Tone		
Pace		
Stereo/mono		
Pitch		
Rhythm		
Tempo		
Melody		
Intensity		
Quality – clear/muffled		
Direction/location		
Continuous/intermittent		
Looping		
Feeling (kinaesthetic)		
Large or small surface area		
Location in body		
Duration		
Breathing rate		
Pulse rate		
Skin temperature		
Weight		
Pressure		
Intensity		

Table 11.1 Continued

Feeling (kinaesthetic)
Still/moving
Rhythm – regular/irregular
Tactile sensations

Smelling and tasting (olfactory and gustatory)
Sweet
Sour
Salt
Bitter
Aroma
Fragrance
Essence
Pungency

Adapted from Bandler (2008a: 79)

fleeting or faint. Individuals can see the picture as though they are looking at everything directly in front of them from 'their own eyes', which is 'associated', and the emotions which accompanied an event can be experienced.

A 'dissociated' perspective derives from looking at a picture or representation within whatever surrounding image there is; this could be like looking at a photograph or a movie of oneself. The emotion associated is less likely to be experienced or is less pronounced. Instead, there may be an emotion of how one feels about observing rather than experiencing the event. A change in 'association' or 'dissociation' can reduce an overwhelming experience of something (associated) to a more objective perspective, which dissociation can bring.

The above exercise elicited the submodalities of a positive and negative experience. Creating a happy or confident state can be as straightforward as eliciting the submodalities from a time when an individual was very happy or confident and simply increasing these submodalities, encouraging the individual to visualise, for example, a more colourful, bigger picture, or increasing the sound, all the while testing to see the impact of these changes. Some submodalities, as discussed earlier, are more crucial to bringing about change; however, it should be remembered that these are individual and context specific. Importantly, individuals who want to visualise can learn to change their own submodalities in the same way.

TIPS FOR SUCCESS

- *Elicit a positive state when required; this is an extremely powerful resource.*
- *Change the attachment and impact of a less than helpful experience. This has not only obvious mental well-being implications, but also leadership and self-management resilience ramifications. Ensure that positive feelings are the dominant, rather than recessive, feature of an individual's thought patterns.*

- *Be aware that negative thoughts can interrupt, cause procrastination and generally influence adversely individuals' ability to function at their best. Having the capability to change this perspective has a potentially positive and significant impact on functionality at work.*
- *Changing or breaking habits also has obvious and important behavioural implications for the leader or manager.*
- *For a change agent the benefits are clear; being able to elicit positive emotional states, particularly in difficult situations, is an asset to all individuals and the teams they work in or with.*
- *Be aware that individuals who are in a positive frame of mind are more apt to challenge appropriately and less liable to accept the status quo (Blanchard, 2007).*
- *Successful interactions with others and developing and maintaining effective networks are increasingly likely to occur when someone has a positive persona and outlook.*
- *Remember that being in a resourceful state is more conducive to problem solving (as interfering mental processing can be reduced or eradicated), with the resultant likelihood of clarity of thought and sound judgement; this establishes a greater intellectual flexibility.*
- *Achieve goal outcomes by creating more compelling attachments using the submodalities; this has clear personal and organisational benefits.*

Section 12
Reframing

This section examines another methodology for changing or reinterpreting problems: 'reframing'.

The term 'reframing' refers to a technique of communication where an individual is helped to reinterpret problems and find solutions by creating another mental frame of reference (Hall, 2001: 238). According to Wake (2010: 73), Gregory Bateson in 1956 was the first person to discuss 'reframes'.

To 'frame' is to put something around another object, in the same way as a photo frame surrounds a photograph or picture. A 'frame' provides a structure to add meaning and definition. Bavister and Vickers (2004: 141) describe a 'frame' as establishing the limitations or constrictions to an event, behaviour or experience, and it is a way in which 'we filter our perceptions based on our internal representation of it', or the meaning attached to an event.

Over time views, beliefs and values have become important rules or 'frames' by which we live, essentially filters, which in positive terms categorise and help us quickly to make sense of situations, information and so on. From a negative perspective, however, these can form habitual thinking or mental ruts which reduce options and alternative choices. All individuals have their favourite 'frames', which can be identified by raising our sensory acuity to them. Clearly, a positive 'frame' or reference requires no challenge; however, a negative frame can stifle productivity and leave individuals feeling 'stuck'.

To reframe is to create a better perspective or a different view of a situation, which can change the meaning and impact, the primary focus being to help an individual to perform more effectively when faced with a perceived limiting belief or problem. Facilitating the adoption of a more useful viewpoint is the main focus of reframing: appreciating an experience in an alternative way or giving it a different significance (Dilts, 1999; O'Connor, 2001). For example, 'We didn't reach an agreement' can be reframed to 'We have an ideal opportunity to readdress this now.' Alder and Heather (1998: 210) suggest that reframing is like refilling, changing the perspective, or deciding to think differently and 'to choose your state of mind'.

Dilts stresses that reframing expands our perception of a situation or event to 'more wisely and resourcefully' handle it. He provides the following example: 'an event that seems unbearably painful when we consider it with respect to our own desires and expectations, for instance, may suddenly seem almost trivial when we compare it to the suffering of others' (1999: 34).

O'Connor and Seymour (2002: 127) describe metaphors and jokes as 'reframing devices'. Events, situations and experiences can, however, create negative emotions; the actual event itself is not the cause but how the individual has chosen to interpret and respond to it. Choosing to look at something in a different way can create new choices, with a positive impact on the emotions. Reframing provides greater flexibility; greater flexibility creates more choices; more choices potentially improve the decision-making process.

Furthermore, changing perception on any given situation allows individuals to have diverse points of view, which can help them to react differently to any given event. By changing your point of view, you begin to transform the meaning, and when that happens you can feel differently about a situation and act differently, with an alternative result or outcome.

Context and content reframes

Reframes can take two forms: context (situation or event) or content (meaning) reframes. Both emphasise looking at something in a different way. Some behaviour has relevance in terms of the content, and some in terms of the context. This presupposes that every behaviour is appropriate in its own way and has value; 'all behaviour is useful in some context' (Tosey and Mathison, 2009: 83). With a context reframe a person takes the disliked behaviour and asks: 'Where could this behaviour be useful?' With a content reframe, the person asks: 'What can this mean to me, and what else could this mean?' Dilts (1999: 40) suggests that 'content reframing involves determining a possible positive intention that could underlie a problematic behaviour'.

EXAMPLES

Context reframe

Statement: *'He's too picky and detailed.'*
Reframed: *'He would make a great project manager.'*

Statement: *'She's too controlling.'*
Reframed: *'She would be great at creating accounts systems and risk management.'*

Content reframe

Statement: *'When I have to present something in public I feel very anxious.'*
Reframed: *'Perhaps this would mean you prepare and perform well.'*

Statement: *'I am always the last to finish work.'*
Reframed: *'You must be thorough and dedicated.'*

Boyes (2006: 126) describes how the following phrases suggest that a context reframe may be required: 'I'm too . . .', 'He's too . . .' or 'I wish I could do this more . . .'

In terms of a content frame that would require reframing you could ask: 'What is it that I or another person has missed or failed to notice?' Content and context reframes can be used at the same time and are not mutually exclusive.

In addition, within NLP, the presupposition guiding principle that individuals make the best choices available to them with their current abilities suggests that there are no unresourceful people, only unresourceful states (see Appendix 2). Indeed, Goleman (1998: 176) discusses the importance of managing one's 'mood', creating an atmosphere of 'openness' and 'neutrality', which he describes as 'essential' for 'good communication' and managing people. Payne and

Cooper (2004) suggest using 'humorous reframing', which is simply using humour; this encourages laughter instead of getting stuck.

Dilts (1999: 43) discusses the importance of reframing with particular reference to 'criticism', which he suggests is linguistically 'generalised judgements', and provides the following examples: 'this proposal is too costly', 'that's not a realistic plan' and 'this project requires too much effort'. The problem with such statements, according to Dilts (1999: 43), is that an individual can 'only agree or disagree' with them, potentially creating a mismatch and conflict if there is no agreement. Reframes offer an alternative response.

Dilts (1999) also reminds us of the fundamental principle, which is linked to the above concept, that an individual makes the best choices, and all behaviours have a positive intention in terms of the deep structure. Examining this intent often can change or reframe the perspective.

EXAMPLES

Negative statement: *'This proposal is too costly.'*
Reframed: *'Be certain that we remain within budget.'*

Negative statement: *'This is a waste of time.'*
Reframed: *'Use available resources wisely.'*

Negative statement: *'Fear of failure.'*
Reframed: *'Desire to succeed.'*

Dilts (1999) suggests however that, once the positive intention of a criticism is defined, the criticism should then be changed into a question, and provides the following examples.

EXAMPLES

Negative statement: *'That idea will never work.'*
Reframed with a question: *'How are you going to actually implement the idea?'*

Negative statement: *That's not a realistic plan.'*
Reframed with a question: *'How can you make the steps of your plan more tangible and concrete?'*

Negative statement: *'It requires too much effort.'*
Reframed with a question: *'How can you make it easier to put into action?'*

This can be summarised in three steps:

1. Find the positive purpose.
2. Make certain the positive intention is identified (framed) positively.
3. Then turn the criticism into a question using 'how' or 'what'; for example: 'What else could this mean?' or 'What would be the opposite way of looking at this?'

It is important when reframing to ensure that rapport has been established to increase the success of application.

Dilts (1999: 52) describes an exercise called 'one-word reframing' that can also help to change an unhelpful perspective. He suggests achieving this by applying the 'one-word reframing' exercise to limiting statements and provides the following example: calling yourself 'stupid' could be reframed by calling yourself 'naive', 'innocent' or 'distracted'. Alder and Heather (1998) remind us that taking a different view can immediately affect not only how someone feels but also the person's behaviour and the overall outcomes.

Cheal's (2008) qualitative study of the role of reframing in the management of organisational paradox suggested that it was an effective problem-solving approach. It is a technique that can be used to address conflict issues for coaching conversations (see Holroyd and Field, 2012) and staff development in terms of challenging a perspective. Reframing arguably resembles lateral, out-of-the-box thinking techniques; however, it is much more and includes the following:

1. Always being open, with a high sensory acuity to detect negative framing in self and others.
2. Increasing self-awareness in the moment to identify potentially 'stuck' frames of thinking.
3. Creating and maintaining rapport when reframing with others.
4. Managing the state to ensure it matches a positive reframe.
5. Ensuring the correct motivational and representational language patterns are matched and used.
6. Always being open to seeing things from a different perspective and creating several reframes.

ACTIVITY **12.1**

Reframing

Identify three perceived problems, issues or events that you would like to reframe using the following questions:

- *What could this mean?*
- *What else could it mean?*
- *Where would this behaviour be useful?*
- *What is the opportunity here?*
- *What would the opposite look like?*

In addition, use 'What if?' and 'How could I?' questions..

TIPS FOR SUCCESS

- *Use reframing when leading changes and developing services, particularly when, as Bradbury (2007: 67) suggests, 70–80 per cent of the population are resistant in some way to change. Your ability to 'reframe' is vital; using an alternative 'frame' can change a negative to a helpful perspective.*
- *Reframing, however, is not an artificial way of looking at things but a way of seeing so-called 'problems' from a number of different perspectives instead of getting stuck with one frame of reference. This flexibility is extremely important in more ways than simply finding*

a better solution or question to ask; it is a healthier mental state to create, for it reduces procrastination and the overwhelming 'stuck' feeling this can produce. Implicitly it generates more choices and in turn increases emotional resilience in managers (Payne and Cooper, 2004).

- *Be aware that there are potential 'natural critics' in all encounters; use this methodology to focus on the useful information a critic identifies without disintegrating into taking things personally, ignoring the individual or having a full-blown confrontation. This provides you, as a manager, with a methodology for success in managing what are often perceived as difficult individuals or encounters.*

- *If you are a manager who is a natural critic, it can help you to put this into perspective, to see things in a different way, to use your talent and then to change the reference point. Furthermore, the example of demonstrating how to manage to 'reframe' something productively is very powerful in terms of you, as a leader, 'leading by example'. Significantly, this role-modelling opportunity potentially has a ripple effect of teaching others how to handle a difficult situation, or individual, effectively.*

- *Boyes (2006: 22) describes the 'outcome frame' in NLP as an important and distinct focus: focusing on the 'outcome' rather than the 'why'. Knowing, for example, 'why' you do something can potentially only provide 'a label' and an ongoing excuse.*

Section 13

Setting well-formed outcomes

In this section we discuss developing an outcome frame, in the form of 'well-formed outcomes' or goals, in more detail. This is an important concept in terms of improving personal and organisational performance.

A well-formed outcome 'is one that has been explored and checked for a number of aspects that will help to improve the likelihood of achieving that outcome' (Youell and Youell, 2011: 56). The 'outcome' is defined as a 'desired state' as distinct from the 'present state'; the emphasis is on being totally clear about what you really want to achieve.

Blanchard (2007: 195) suggests that change is necessary when 'there is a discrepancy between an actual set of events, and a desired set of events – what you would like to happen'. Outcome thinking and making things materialise come naturally to some people, while others procrastinate, focusing instead on what is wrong and who or what can be blamed.

Evading problems and the propensity to focus on moving away from potential pain are a pattern learnt from childhood (Jacobson, 1996). He contrasts this with the more productive stance of moving 'towards goals or pleasure' and being in a 'solution state' to attain the desired outcome(s).

Setting goals or outcomes implies there is a solution or a more effective way (Wake, 2010: 27). Wake (2010) also cites Solms's evidence from 1996 that the system responsible for self-regulation, organised mental activity and the stimulation of towards motivation states, the reticular activation system (RAS), is stimulated by goal setting. This is a natural process of development activated from as early as three months of age (Stern, cited in Wake, 2010: 29).

The following statement may be familiar: 'If you don't know where you are going to, how do you know when you've arrived?' It seems a wise statement in relation to goal and objective setting. However, if you applied well-formed outcomes principles this statement would be revised to: 'If you cannot specifically define your precise destination, how do you really know that you want to go there in the first place?'

Setting well-formed outcomes

Well-formed outcomes can be applied to:

- individual or personal aspirations or goals;
- team objectives or goals;
- peer objectives or goals;
- organisational objectives.

Developing well-formed outcomes focuses on stating what you want rather than being distracted by trying to solve a problem or problems (Bradbury, 2007).

Knowing clearly what you desire is an important part – the results gained in life are predominantly what someone has generated. For example, individuals recognise more easily references which confirm and support their beliefs or expectations. A continuation of this perspective would suggest, therefore, that to succeed individuals have to presume and believe that they are going to succeed (Bradbury, 2007: 37).

O'Connor and Seymour suggest:

The more precisely and positively you can define what you want, and the more you programme your brain to seek out and notice possibilities, the more likely you are to get what you want. Opportunities exist when they are recognised as opportunities.

(2002: 10)

McMaster and Grinder (1993) also emphasise, in terms of successful realisation, the importance of defining the difference between the present and the desired states as precisely as possible.

The process of attaining outcomes is described as a 'journey' from the 'present state' to a 'desired state', with the resources required being identified (O'Connor and Seymour, 2002: 12). Importantly, O'Connor and Seymour refer to an individual's behaviours, thoughts and feelings as being different in the present state compared to the desired state, and the significance of identifying these is stressed as a condition for achieving the outcomes.

Identifying an outcome creates a 'difference' in two states: the present and the desired. O'Connor (2001: 11) delineates an outcome as different to a 'task', which he refers to as what you have to do to attain an 'outcome'.

O'Connor (2001: 12) describes four provisional questions to pose in order to make the so-called 'journey' a success:

1. What am I moving towards? *(the desired state or outcome)*
2. Why am I moving? *(the guiding values)*
3. How will I get there? *(the strategy for the journey)*
4. What if something goes wrong? *(risk management and contingency planning)*

O'Connor (2001: 14) describes the resources (see Figure 13.1) as: 'mental strategies, life experiences, personal qualities, skills, language, physiology, emotional states, beliefs and values'. Youell and Youell (2011: 61) add determination and confidence. Other obvious resources include financial resources, materials and products of any description, for example software.

The question to ask is which resources are already available and which need to be attained, for example, training and development. Furthermore, under what circumstances have outcomes like this been achieved before, and what resources, such as experience, can be drawn upon?

Table 13.1 depicts Figure 13.1 with an additional perspective called 'objections'. The objections in Table 13.1 identify the hazards to the outcome and would typically include the risks.

O'Connor (2001: 18) stresses that an individual needs to 'believe three things' about their outcomes:

1. it is possible to achieve them;
2. the individual is able to achieve them; and
3. the individual deserves to achieve them.

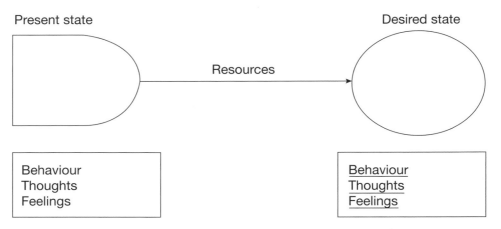

Figure 13.1 The components of setting well-formed outcomes

Table 13.1 Present and desired states

Present state (what you see, hear and feel)	Desired state (what you see, hear and feel)
Objections	Resources

Self-rehearsal

This would encompass practising or rehearsing and could be achieved through visualisation or running through something that needs to be said. Politis (2005), in his study of self-management, found that self-rehearsal was an important factor for both creativity and improving performance.

Boyes (2006: 87) described something similar, which she refers to as 'mental rehearsal'. An important distinction in this case is, when visualising achieving the outcome, to notice any 'self-talk' which may reveal underlying 'limiting beliefs'.

Identifying the first steps

Transforming an outcome into something that is achieved requires taking action; identifying the first step is a 'key stage' in the well-formed outcome process. Indeed, Bavister and Vickers (2004: 81) advocate that the most important part is defining 'the first step'. Changing an 'outcome into a reality requires action'. Bavister and Vickers (2004) describe defining this first step as the final, and a significant, aspect of the 'well-formedness condition'. Establishing and taking the first step are also a good indicator of the level of motivation associated with the outcome. Breaking something down into identifiable steps is always a helpful approach, and completing the first step is an important reinforcement for continuing the progress to realise the outcome.

In defining well-formed outcomes the following checklist has some important considerations to take into account.

'Well-formedness' checklist

The following checklist has been adapted from a number of authors: Alder and Heather (1998); Hayes (2006); and Youell and Youell (2011). Each identified outcome should satisfy the following criteria.

1. Use positive terms to define the outcome

This relates to the desired state or destination: the defined outcome. It is stated in the positive; as discussed earlier, the brain cannot process a negative. This is the 'what you want' rather than the 'what you don't want'. For example, 'reducing financial waste' could be replaced by 'achieving better management of resources' or 'increasing productivity'.

Focus simply on what is the desired outcome. Thinking about what is not wanted and even considering the process, the 'how to', will distract from describing precisely the outcomes. It was established earlier that language can create powerful visual imagery – an important consideration when expressing the outcome. Defining something concentrates the thoughts and thinking and opens a programme or file in the mind; this is the direction of travel; this is to be achieved.

Useful prompt questions

- What is really or most wanted?
- Attaining this will . . .?
- What is to be changed?
- What will be achieved?
- What will be gained?

2. Be specific

This is about being as specific and precise as possible. The more explicitly and precisely it is stated, the more likely it is that the exact outcome will be achieved. Language, in terms of the written form, can be limiting; there are only so many words, and individuals and organisations have their favourite phrases, expressions and constructs. Defining an outcome is a process of deleting, potentially distorting and generalising. Being clear and checking the interpretation of each word are vital steps in the process.

Remember, 'nominalisations', verbs turned into nouns, change a process word into a 'non-action' word, producing the sensation of being 'stuck'. This is not a desired position in terms of achieving goals.

Useful prompt questions

- Is this language that anyone can understand?
- Are there alternative meanings for the words used which could create confusion?
- Are there any nominalisations?
- What is it specifically that will denote that the outcome has been achieved? What else? And what else?

3. Be sensory-specific

The outcome is imagined in specific detail using all five senses (what it will look, sound, feel, smell and taste like). This is about creating sufficient detail to make it tangible and convincing. Alder and Heather (1998: 23) suggest that this process can trigger 'associations' and 'insights' into the 'how to achieve'. Using sensory-specific terms stimulates the reticular activation system, which triggers the 'arousal and attention responses' (Wake, 2010: 32).

The outcome has been achieved now; what would that feel like, what can you see, what can you hear and what are you telling yourself? If this is a peer group objective, visualise what each individual will look like, the expressions on their faces, the tone in their voices, what they are saying, the specific words they will use, what you are saying and what is particularly important to you. Alder and Heather (1998: 23) suggest that 'vivid sensory representations of an outcome set up a sequence of neural associations', and these 'steer . . . from inner experience to external reality'.

Useful prompt questions

- What will you see?
- What will you feel?
- What will you hear?
- What will you be telling yourself?

4. Use evidence

Evidence is required to demonstrate that:

- an outcome has been achieved;
- the right direction is being maintained, as an ongoing feedback process;
- measures can relate to 'self' and others.

This is linked to the sensory-specific criteria mentioned above, as the evidence ought to resemble the original visualised and sensory-imagined outcomes. The evidence should also have a quantifiable and measurable output. Hayes (2006: 87) suggests that, 'the more evidence for success you are able to describe, the more compelling it will be'.

It is important to gather evidence of progress towards the desired outcome to ensure the right direction is being maintained. This may be in the form of defined milestones with specific and realistic review dates.

Useful prompt questions

- How will you know you have achieved the outcome(s)?
- How will you know exactly when you have achieved the outcome(s)?
- What specifically will you see, hear and feel when the outcome is attained?
- What specific feedback will you need, and when, to ensure you are still heading in the right direction?
- How will you measure your progress?
- What are your defined milestones?

5. Keep control

It is important that the goal is within the individual's control, even if collaboration with others is necessary. This is about what you can do and be responsible for. Importantly, it relates back to the concept of only truly being able to change 'self'.

If the outcome involves others, this is about being absolutely clear what you are individually responsible for and, more specifically, what is within your power. This includes what you can influence. Alder and Heather (1998: 26) suggest 'control the controllable and let the rest take care of itself'.

Useful prompt questions

- What is my specific role in achieving this outcome?
- What will achieving this outcome mean to me?
- What difference will attaining this outcome make to me?
- What matters to me?
- How will I specifically affect this outcome?
- What can I control?
- Is any assistance required to achieve this outcome?

6. Who is involved?

This links with the above criteria about being particularly clear who is involved and the individual responsibilities. This is about establishing roles and responsibilities and also appreciating not only whom you need to report to, but also whom you can ask for help. It is important to establish who is responsible for starting and whether this is different from who is responsible for maintaining the outcome.

Useful prompt questions

- What matters to each individual or group affected?
- Who can and who will help?
- What part of the outcome belongs to other individuals?
- Would other individuals need to be influenced and motivated to achieve the desired outcome?
- Who is responsible for the maintenance, if this is appropriate?

7. Contextualise

This is the 'where', 'when', 'what', 'how' and 'with whom' the outcome is realised. The change may be required only in certain contexts, which therefore need to be specified. In what context is the outcome appropriate or not? If there is any delegation, is it clear what and to whom?

It also involves what is included and what is not, specifically where the boundaries are. An outcome which works well in one environment or arena may not work so well in another. This can be a perpetual problem within the public sector services, where a great outcome in one arena or part of the country is imposed as the latest idea and, not surprisingly, the impact is different in the new context. Being more assertive as an outcome may be appropriate at work; however, at home it may potentially cause conflict.

Useful prompt questions

- What is the specific context?
- When is this outcome appropriate?
- Where is this outcome appropriate?
- What is this outcome appropriate for?
- How is this outcome appropriate?
- For whom is this outcome appropriate?

8. Consider the financial implications

This includes looking at what financial resources are required and how these requirements might have an impact on the wider context. Is value for money created? Is it worth the financial investment? When compared to other outcomes, in order of importance, how do the financial implications have an impact, and has this outcome been assessed in this way?

Useful prompt questions

- Are there any financial consequences attached to the outcome?
- Have these been measured and quantified?
- What are the wider financial ramifications?
- Have these been accurately assessed?
- Has a cost–benefit analysis been undertaken?

9. Maintain positive by-products

In achieving the goal or outcome it is important to identify if anything will be lost or significantly compromised. Any advantage or positive elements of the present state which need to be transferred to the desired state should be identified and not lost. The impact on other outcomes also needs to be cross-checked for the potential loss of positive elements.

In the rush to implement good ideas, and the related outcomes, the cost is sometimes significant in terms of losing existing benefits. However, in other scenarios there can be a secondary gain which may affect the success or otherwise of the outcome. Invariably, an individual receives a gain from a negative action or behaviour; changing this may be more problematic, especially if it is undetected. It could be important to find a replacement for the secondary gain to ensure the outcome is not sabotaged.

Useful prompt questions

- Are there any positive benefits which may be unintentionally lost with this outcome?
- Will there be a loss of something that you would want to keep?
- What other impact or effects will this outcome have, and are these all advantageous?
- Is there any obvious secondary gain, and how can this be appropriately replaced?

10. Consider the time implications

Have the real time considerations been thoroughly thought through? Timescales are something that should always be specified and clear. People who are optimistic may produce impossible deadlines, and the converse is true of naturally pessimistic individuals.

In addition, is this outcome appropriately timed, or would it be better to delay to improve its success? This is also about ensuring that other planned desired outcomes are not adversely affected by this current outcome.

Useful prompt questions

- What timescale is achievable?
- What timescale is realistic?
- Precisely how long will it take?
- When do you want to achieve the outcome?
- Could the best outcome be achieved by [date]?
- Are there any other outcomes which could delay the implementation?

11. Consider ecology (is it worth it?)

As discussed above, the outcome must be worth the cost in every sense, not just the money and time. A well-formed outcome does not have an adverse impact on things that are important to the individual; it should instead enhance these. This refers to the wider systems which individuals operate within, such as family, friends, relationships, teams, the organisation, peer groups, networks, other organisations and the community. For example, increasing your work commitments to achieve an outcome can have an impact on the family unit, especially if the work requires more hours.

The ecology is about assessing the advantages and disadvantages in relation to this larger system. This is an opportunity to stand back and look at the total impact and ascertain how achieving the desired outcomes might affect others and whether there are any unintended results.

No matter how small the outcome it will have consequential impacts; some will be obvious, others will need more considered analysis to anticipate, and a few will not be known. This consideration applies to the process as well as the achievement of the outcome.

McMaster and Grinder (1993) suggest that an example of an ecology fit is making sure that outcomes developed lower down in the organisation take into account any goals and objectives at a higher level.

Useful prompt questions

- Is this me? Does it feel right?
- Am I certain this is what I want?
- Are my identity and aspirations captured within this outcome?

- What are the time implications?
- Is this outcome appropriate in all situations?
- Does gaining this outcome achieve choice?
- What additional outcome does this take me towards?
- Does the outcome support the fuller sense of self?
- What would not happen if the outcomes were achieved?
- What would happen if the outcomes were not achieved?
- What would not happen if the outcomes were not achieved?
- What will happen if the outcomes are achieved?

12. Act 'as if'

This is similar to the 'What if?' or scenario planning approaches in projects; for example, 'What if the funding arrangements suddenly changed and there was a 50 per cent deficit?' A number of potential scenarios are identified in the same way to elicit and explore areas which may have been overlooked.

This also allows an individual to take on a particular stance or role to provide further insights. For example, what would the finance director say, or the head of human resources?

Useful prompt questions

- What would happen if . . .?
- What would it be like when . . .?
- Imagine being the project lead; what would that person say?
- What if you were a service user?
- What if you had a magic wand?
- What if you stepped into the future and looked back; what would this mean?

EXAMPLE OF A WELL-FORMED OUTCOME

I have completed all the initial children's assessments within the permitted time (10 working days) for 12 consecutive months. I am looking at the spreadsheet detailing this evidence. My manager is saying well done. This improvement means that the whole team has met this objective and so there are lots of smiling faces. This is a realistic and attainable goal. I have the ability, the know-how, the resources, and the support of my colleagues. I do need to look at the current daily distractions. My first step is to map and identify these.

Well-formedness criteria

Table 13.2 summarises the well-formedness criteria and compares these to the SMART criteria associated with determining objectives.

Table 13.2 SMART objectives and well-formed outcomes compared

SMART objectives	Well-formed outcomes
Specific	Positively stated
Measurable	Specific
Attainable	Sensory-specific
Realistic	Evidence
Timely	Control
	'Who' (responsible/involved/can help)
	Context
	Financial considerations
	Positive by-products
	Time considerations
	'Ecology'
	Acting 'as if'

Why outcomes are more effective than objectives

Molden (2007) argues that developing outcomes is far more productive than creating objectives, which he believes focuses simply on the achievement and does not take into consideration the wider impact of potential consequences and the 'ecology'.

The attainment of the outcome or goal must be perceived to be worthwhile and realisable. O'Connor (2001: 11) makes the distinction that, unlike objectives, NLP outcomes are characterised by the thorough assessment against particular specifications which make them 'realistic, motivating and achievable'.

In organisations, objectives are set and action plans developed and progressed through tasks that are soon relinquished as the original realistic targets quickly become unrealistic, and a lack of specificity creates procrastination; distractions then steal the motivation which once fuelled the initial creation and dedication to the plan. Loss of faith in the plan is soon followed by failure. A creeping sense that objective setting is a bureaucratic task that is sabotaged by 'reality' may be a reasoned conclusion. Not all of the above may have been experienced. However, most individuals can relate to goals and objectives not achieving everything they had planned.

Using the advanced questioning skills to elicit the potentially missing details would be a successful approach. Field (in Gray, Field and Brown, 2010) also advocates the importance of developing well-formed outcomes, alluding to the need to ensure that wider and fuller considerations are accessed as part of the process to avoid becoming too narrowly focused.

Jacobson (1996: 7) adds that the results should be 'tested against some measurable standard' and that the learning gained should be captured and 'used in the future'. He also suggests that outcomes should be aligned with an individual's values. Covey (1992) adds holding people to account as an important element to ensuring success.

Another important area, often neglected at the expense of organisational commitment, is the development of personal outcomes.

A focus on personal outcomes

When it comes to identifying personal goals, deciding on well-thought-through outcomes can be difficult. Expectations can get in the way; someone who may have low self-esteem, or is stressed, can be caught up in procrastinating over what is important to 'self'. Staying busy can temporarily stop the self-analysis, and the awareness that this is not sustainable in the long term. It is therefore important to ask the following:

- 'What makes me happy?'
- 'What is important?'
- 'Have I got time for me?'
- 'Have I taken so many things on that I am competing with myself?'

Table 13.3 may help in identifying what is important. Categorise things in each of the columns. For example, 'I have a car, and I want a car'; 'I don't have a dog, but I want one'; 'I have a busy schedule, and I don't want this'; and 'I don't have a sports car, and I don't want one either.' Moving the items from the columns 'I don't have/I want' and 'I have/I don't want' will help to determine what you truly want as a goal or outcome.

Table 13.3 Goal setting

I have I want	I don't have I want	I have I don't want	I don't have I don't want
A car	A dog	A busy schedule	A sports car

TIPS FOR SUCCESS

- *Molden (2007: 51) describes having goals and outcomes as 'the very essence of management activity'. Others (Covey, 1992; Goleman 1998; Lee, 2007) stress the importance of goals and outcomes for personal growth, lifelong learning and, in particular, maintaining continuous professional development.*
- *Blanchard (2007) emphasises the significance of ensuring that all individuals at work have clear goals rather than presume they know what they are doing. He suggests that this is key to 'good performance', together with providing specific feedback in relation to the attainment or otherwise of the desired outcomes.*
- *Yukl (1998) would concur, suggesting that there is clear evidence that goal setting results in higher performance. Senge et al. (1999) add the importance of aligning personal and organisational goals to increase their realisation and impact.*

And simply to say . . .

Remember, 'true leadership' is about being ethical in all that you do. While the strategies detailed in this book are powerful ones that really do make a difference, moment by moment, they should be applied with the utmost integrity. It is up to you, your choice.

Appendix 1

National Occupational Standards for management and leadership

In 2005 (reviewed in 2008) the Management Standards Centre detailed the following management standards covering six function areas:

Function area

Function A	Managing self and personal skills
Function B	Providing direction
Function C	Facilitating change
Function D	Working with people
Function E	Using resources
Function F	Achieving results

Appendix 2

'Presuppositions' as guiding principles

The following are a number of 'presuppositions' in NLP which can be used as guiding principles. Hayes (2006: 19) suggests that each stands alone as helpful. However, they are even more 'powerful when linked together to create a framework and structure of mutually reinforcing attitudes and assumptions'.

- **The positive worth of the individual is held constant, while the value and appropriateness of internal and/or external behaviour are questioned.**
  People are not 'broken' and don't need to be 'fixed'; their behaviour is useful or not useful and based on individual strategies that may be less effective. O'Connor (2001) suggests focusing, if appropriate, on changing the strategy to something more useful and effective.
- **There is no failure, only feedback. All results and behaviours are achievements, whether or not they are desired outcomes for a given task or context.**
  When you can learn from each mistake, you can see mistakes as feedback, which can be used to improve performance; it is all part of the learning process.
- **The resources individuals need to effect a change are already within them.**
  All individuals have the ability to change their thoughts, feelings, beliefs and behaviours, and therefore they have all the resources to change. The key is how to learn to use these resources to create a permanent change.
- **Underlying all behaviour there is a positive intention for that individual.**
  NLP does not claim that all behaviour is necessarily the best possible choice from an objective point of view, or that it will have positive benefits for everyone. It focuses on separating the intention behind the action from the action or behaviour. As O'Connor (2001: 228) states, 'A person is not their behaviour.'
- **The meaning of the communication is the response you get.**
  The success of the communication depends on the communicator. Taking responsibility for your own communication and its effects will provide a much better chance of succeeding than blaming any misunderstandings on those you are communicating with. Furthermore, remember that we are communicating all the time both verbally and non-verbally.
- **Respecting other people's different models of the world creates greater behavioural flexibility.**
  This flexibility allows individuals to bridge the gap between their way of thinking and somebody else's, which enables them to communicate more effectively with the other person.

- **People will normally make the best choices available to them.**
  People within their current resources, experiences and abilities will make the best choices they can until they are aware of new options. Creating an increased number of choices and options creates greater flexibility.
- **Everyone has a unique model (map) of the world.**
  Individuals have different past experiences, values and beliefs, which provide them with their so-called 'map of the world'. It is their 'map' and not 'reality' itself; it is a view or perception and, according to Boyes (2006: 18), 'changing how you see the world (your map) you will be able to change the results you get in that world'.
- **All information is processed through our senses.**
  We make sense of the world through our five senses: through internal images, internal sounds, talking to ourselves, gut feelings and our personal interpretation of tastes and smells. Problems are strategies and are made up from the way we represent the world and therefore can be broken down and changed.
- **Mind and body form one system.**
  Our thoughts affect our physiology. When we change either mind or body, we change the other. Altering our thoughts cannot change behaviour and also the associated physiology.
- **Rapport determines the success in communicating with another person.**
  The level of rapport you have with someone will determine the success or otherwise in communicating a specific message.
- **If you want to understand, act.**
  You do not really understand something until you have actually done it yourself. 'We forget what we hear, remember what we see and understand what we do' (based on Confucius, 551–479 BC).

Appendix 3
Parts of speech

Part of speech	Function	Examples
Verb	Action or state.	To be, have, do, can, shiver, boil, bangs, run.
Noun	Thing or person.	Cat, ball, Manchester, Richard, toothpaste, car, music, shop, card, telephone.
Pronoun	Replaces a noun.	I, me, she, he, him, her, they, them, we, us, it.
Adverb	Describes or tells us more about the meaning of a verb.	Loudly, slowly, brightly, angrily, happily, early, hardly.
Adjective	Describes a noun.	Large, nice, interesting, awful, rather, graceful, red, loud, smart, great.
Conjunction	Joins clauses or sentences; connects other words or groups of words.	Because, when, and, but, or, so, as, since, than, while, until, although, if.
Preposition	Links a noun to another word.	On, to, at, after, by, under, for, in, near, across.

References

Alder, H. (1996) *NLP for Managers: How to Achieve Excellence at Work*. London: Piatkus.

Alder, H. and Heather, B. (1998) *NLP in 21 Days: A Complete Introduction and Training Programme*. London: Piatkus.

Alimo-Metcalfe, B. and Alban-Metcalfe, J. (2005) The crucial role of leadership in meeting the challenges of change. *Vision: The Journal of Business Perspective*, 9(2), April–June: 27–39.

Anderson, M.C., Ochsner, K.N., Kuhl, B., Cooper, J., Robertson, E., Gabrieli, S.W., Glover, G.H. and Gabrieli, J.D.E. (2004) Neural systems underlying the suppression of unwanted memories. *Science*, 303(5655), 9 January: 232–5.

Argyle, M. (1994) *The Psychology of Interpersonal Behaviour*. London: Penguin Books.

Argyle, M., Salter, V., Nicholson, H., Williams, M. and Burgess, P. (1970) The communication of inferior and superior attitudes by verbal and non-verbal signals. *British Journal of Social and Clinical Psychology*, 9: 222–31.

Arnsten, A.F.T. (2009) Stress signalling pathways that impair prefrontal cortex structure and function. *Nature Reviews Neuroscience*, 10, June: 410–22.

Avolio, B.J., Walumbwa, F.O. and Weber, T.J. (2009) Leadership: Current theories, research, and future directions. *Annual Review of Psychology*, 60: 421–49.

Bandler, R. (2008a) *Get the Life You Want: The Secrets to Lasting Life Change*. Deerfield Beach, FL: Health Communications.

Bandler, R. (2008b) *Guide to Trance-Formation*. Deerfield Beach, FL: Health Communications.

Bandler, R. and Grinder, J. (1975a) *The Structure of Magic*. Palo Alto, CA: Science and Behavior Books.

Bandler, R. and Grinder, J. (1975b) *Patterns of Hypnotic Techniques of Milton H. Erickson, MD*, vol 1. Scotts Valley, CA: Grinder & Associates.

Bandler, R. and MacDonald, W. (1988) *An Insider's Guide to Sub-Modalities*. Capitola, CA: Meta Publications.

Bandler, R. and La Valle, J. (2002) *Charisma Enhancement and Trainer Training*. Hopatcong, NJ: NLP Seminars Group International.

Bass, B.M. and Steidlmeier, P. (1999) Ethics, character, and authentic transformation leadership behaviour. *Leadership Quarterly*, 10: 181–217.

Bavister, S. and Vickers, A. (2004) *Essential NLP*. London: Teach Yourself.

Benedict, C. (2008) For the brain remembering is reliving. *New York Times*, 4 September, http://www.nytimes.com/2008/09/05/science/05brain.html.

Bennett, M.P., Zeller, J.M., Rosenberg, L. and McCann, J. (2003) The effect of mirthful laughter on stress and natural killer cell activity. *Alternative Therapies in Health and Medicine*, March–April.

Bennis, W. and Nanus, N. (1985) *Leaders: The Strategies for Taking Charge*. New York: Harper & Row.

Blanchard, K. (2007) *Leading at a Higher Level: Blanchard on How to Be a High Performing Leader*. Harlow: FT Prentice Hall.

Bodenhamer, B.G. and Hall, L.M. (1997) *Figuring Out People: Design Engineering with Meta-Programs*. Bancyfelin, Carmarthen: Anglo American Books.

Bolden, R., Gosling, J., Marturano, A. and Dennison, P. (2003) *A Review of Leadership Theory and Competency Frameworks*. Exeter: Centre for Leadership Studies, University of Exeter.

Bolstad, R. (2002) *Resolve: A New Model of Therapy*. Bancyfelin, Carmarthen: Crown House Publishing.

Borg, J. (2008) *Body Language: 7 Easy Lessons to Master the Silent Language*. Harlow: Pearson Education.

Boyes, C. (2006) *Need to Know? NLP*. London: Collins.

Bradbury, A. (2007) *Develop Your NLP Skills*. London: Sunday Times/Kogan Page.

Bradbury, A. (2010) *Develop Your NLP Skills*, 4th edn. London: Sunday Times/Kogan Page.

Brandis, A. (1987) A neurolinguistic treatment for reducing parental anger responses and creating more resourceful behavioural options. California School of Professional Psychology, Los Angeles, Dissertation abstract. *Dissertation Abstracts International*, 47(11-B), May: 4642.

Braye, R.H. (2002) Servant-leadership: Leading in today's military, in Spears, L.C. and Lawrence, M. (eds), *Focus on Leadership: Servant-Leadership for the 21st Century*. New York: John Wiley & Sons.

Brockman, W. (1981) Empathy revisited: The effect of representational system matching on certain counselling process and outcome variables. Doctoral dissertation, College of William and Mary, 1980. *Dissertation Abstracts International*, 41: 3421A (University Microfilms No. 81-035: 91).

Cheal, J. (2008) Exploring the role of NLP in the management of organisational paradox. *Current Research in NLP*, 1 (Proceedings of 2008 Conference): 33–48.

Cheal, J. (2010) The role of moods in NLP. *Enhancing and Advancing Neuro Linguistic Programming: A New Anthology of Shared Findings and Learnings*, 1(1), November: 28–36.

Chomsky, N. (1957) *Syntactic Structure*. The Hague: Mouton.

Churches, R. and Terry, R. (2010) *NLP for Teachers*. Bancyfelin, Carmarthen: Crown House Publishing.

CIPD (2008) *NLP at Work*. March, www.cipd.co.uk/subjects/maneco/general/nlp.

Covey, S. (1992) *Principle Centred Leadership*. London: Simon & Schuster UK.

Cowan, N. (2001) The magical number 4 in short-term memory: A reconsideration of mental storage capacity. *Behavioural and Brain Science*, 24: 87–185.

Dilts, R.B. (1999) *Sleight of Mouth: The Magic of Conversational Belief Change*. Capitola, CA: Meta Publications.

Dispenza, J. (2007) *Evolve Your Brain: The Science of Changing Your Mind*. Deerfield Beach, FL: Health Communications.

Dompke, U. (2001) Human behaviour representation – definition, in Research and Technology Organisation (RTO) of NATO, *Simulation of and for Military Decision Making*, RTO-EN-017, RTO SAS Lecture Series 222. Neuilly-sur-Seine: RTO.

Doughty, M.J. (2002) Further assessment of gender and blink pattern related differences in the spontaneous eye blink activity in primary gaze in young adult humans. *Optometry and Vision Science*, 79(7), July: 439–47.

Ekman, P. (2003) *Emotions Revealed: Understanding Faces and Feelings*. London: Phoenix.

Ekman, P. and Friesen, W.V. (2003) *Unmasking the Face: A Guide to Recognising Emotions from Facial Expressions*. Los Altos, CA: Malor Books.

Feder, A., Nestler, E.J. and Charney, D.S. (2009) Psychobiology and molecular genetics of resilience. *Nature Reviews Neuroscience*, 10, June: 446–57.

Gardner, W., Avolio, B., Luthans, F., Walumbwa, F. and May, D. (2005) 'Can you see the real me?' A self-based model of authentic leader and follower development. *Leadership Quarterly*, 16(3): 343–72.

Goldberg, E. (2009) *The New Executive Brain: Frontal Lobes in a Complex World*. Oxford: Oxford University Press.

Goleman, D. (1998) *Working with Emotional Intelligence*. London: Bloomsbury Publishing.

Goleman, D. (2000) Leadership that gets results. *Harvard Business Review*, March–April.

Goleman, D. (2002) *The New Leaders: Transforming the Art of Leadership into the Science of Results*. London: Little, Brown.

Gray, I., Field, R. and Brown, K. (2010) *Effective Leadership, Management and Supervision in Health and Social Care*. Exeter: Learning Matters.

Hafford-Letchfield, T. (2007) *Practising Quality Assurance in Social Care*. Exeter: Learning Matters.

Hall, J. (1984) *Nonverbal Sex Differences: Communication Accuracy and Expressive Style*. Baltimore, MD: Johns Hopkins University Press.

Hall, L.M. (2001) *Communication Magic: Exploring the Structure and Meaning of Language*. Bancyfelin, Carmarthen: Crown House Publishing.

Hall, L.M. (2007) *The Sourcebook of Magic: A Comprehensive Guide to NLP Change Patterns*, 2nd edn. Bancyfelin, Carmarthen: Crown House Publishing.

Hayes, P. (2006) *NLP Coaching: Coaching in Practice*. Maidenhead: Open University Press, McGraw-Hill Education.

Hayes, P. (2008) *NLP Coaching: Coaching in Practice*. Maidenhead: Open University Press, McGraw-Hill Education.

Hock, D. (2002) Leadership and the chaordic age, in Spears, L.C. and Lawrence, M. (eds), *Focus on Leadership: Servant-Leadership for the 21st Century*. New York: John Wiley & Sons.

Holroyd, J. and Brown, K. (2011) *Leadership and Management Development for Social Work and Social Care: Creating Leadership Pathways of Progression*. Bournemouth: Learn to Care/Bournemouth University.

Holroyd, J. and Field, R. (2012) *Performance Coaching Skills for Social Work*. London: Sage.

Holroyd, J. and Ross, V. (2011) *Introduction to Leadership and Management: Improving Personal and Organisational Performance*. Bournemouth: Bournemouth University.

Howard, C. (2011) Results certificates version 5. Christopher Howard Training.

Jacobson, S. (1996) *Solution States: A Course in Solving Problems in Business with the Power of NLP*. Bancyfelin, Carmarthen: Crown House Publishing.

Katzenbach, J.R. and Smith, D.K. (1993) *The Wisdom of Teams: Creating the High-Performance Organization*. Boston, MA: Harvard Business School Press.

Kaufman, J., Plotsky, P.M., Nemeroff, C.B. and Charney, D.S. (2000) Effects of early adverse experiences on brain structure and function: Clinical implications. *Society of Biological Psychiatry*, 48: 778–90.

Kehoe, J. (2010) *Mind Power into the 21st Century: Techniques to Harness the Astounding Powers of Thought*. Vancouver: Zoetic.

Klenke, K. (2005) The internal theater of the authentic leader: Integrating cognitive, affective, conative and spiritual facets of authentic leadership, in Gardner, W., Avolio, B. and Walumbwa, F. (eds), *Authentic Leadership Theory and Practice: Origins, Effects and Development*, pp. 155–82. Oxford: Elsevier.

Kloet, E.R. de, Joels, M. and Holsboer, F. (2005) Stress and the brain: From adaptation to disease. *Nature Reviews Neuroscience*, 6, June: 463–75.

Korzybski, A. (1933) *Science and Sanity: An Introduction to Non-Aristotelian Systems and General Semantics*, 1st edn. New York: Institute of General Semantics.

Korzybski, A. (1948) *Science and Sanity: An Introduction to Non-Aristotelian Systems and General Semantics*, 3rd edn. New York: Institute of General Semantics.

Korzybski, A. (1994) *Science and Sanity: An Introduction to Non-Aristotelian Systems and General Semantics*, 5th edn. New York: Institute of General Semantics.

Kouzes, J.M. and Posner, B.Z. (2007) *The Leadership Challenge*, 4th edn. San Francisco: Jossey-Bass.

Lakoff, G. and Johnson, M. (1999) *Philosophy in the Flesh*. New York: Basic Books.

Lawley, J. and Tompkins, P. (2000) *Metaphors in Mind*. London: Developing Company Press.

Lazarus, J. (2010) *Successful NLP: For the Results You Want*. Richmond, Surrey: Crimson.

Lee, G. (2007) *Leadership Coaching: From Personal Insight to Organisational Performance*. London: CIPD.

Lewis, S., Passmore, J. and Cantore, S. (2009) *Appreciative Inquiry for Change Management: Using AI to Facilitate Organisational Development*. London: Kogan Page.

Linder-Pelz, S. (2010) *NLP Coaching: An Evidence-Based Approach for Coaches, Leaders and Individuals*. London: Kogan Page.

McDermott, I. and Jago, W. (2003) *The NLP Coach: A Comprehensive Guide to Personal Well-Being and Professional Success*. London: Piatkus.

McEwen, B.S. (2000) The neurobiology of stress: from serendipity to clinical relevance. *Brain Research*, 886: 172–89.

McMaster, M. and Grinder, J. (1993) *Precision: A New Approach to Communication – How to Get the Information You Need to Get the Results*. Scotts Valley, CA: Grinder, DeLozier and Associates.

Medina, J. (2008) *Brain Rules: 12 Principles for Surviving and Thriving at Work, Home and School*. Seattle, WA: Pear Press.

Miller, G.A. (1956) The magical number seven, plus or minus two: Some limits on our capacity for processing information. *Psychological Review*, 63, 81–97.

Molden, D. (2001) *NLP Business Masterclass*. Harlow: Pearson Education.

Molden, D. (2007) *Managing with the Power of NLP: A Model for Better Management*, 2nd edn. Harlow: Pearson Education.

Monti, D. (2000) The mind–body connection: The effects of thought on the body, transcribed from *What the Bleep!? Down the Rabbit Hole*. London: Revolver Entertainment.

Morgan, G. (2006) *Images of Organization*. Thousand Oaks, CA: Sage.

Navarro, J. (2008) *What Every Body Is Saying*. New York: HarperCollins.

Neck, C.P. and Manz, C.C. (2009) *Mastering Self-Leadership: Empowering Yourself for Personal Excellence*. Englewood Cliffs, NJ: Prentice Hall.

Neill, M. (2009) *Supercoach: 10 Secrets to Transform Anyone's Life*. London: Hay House.

NHS (2004) *The Leadership and Qualities Framework*. London: Department of Health.

O'Connor, J. (2001) *NLP Workbook: A Practical Guide to Achieving the Results You Want*. London: HarperCollins.

O'Connor, J. and Seymour, J. (2002) *Introducing NLP: Psychological Skills for Understanding and Influencing People*. London: Harper Element.

O'Connor, J. and Lages, A. (2004) *Coaching with NLP: A Practical Guide to Getting the Best Out of Yourself and Others*. London: HarperCollins.

Patterson, K., Grenny, J., McMillan, R. and Switzler, A. (2002) *Crucial Conversations: Tools for Talking When Stakes Are High*. Maidenhead: McGraw-Hill.

Payne, R.L. and Cooper, C.L. (2004) *Emotions at Work: Theory, Research and Applications for Management*. Chichester: John Wiley & Sons.

Peters, T. and Waterman, R.H. (2004) *In Search of Excellence*. London: Profile Books.

Politis, J.D. (2005) Dispersed leadership predictor of the work environment for creativity and productivity. *European Journal of Innovation Management*, 8(2): 182–204.

Pransky, J. (2003) *Prevention from the Inside-Out*. Cabot, VT: 1st Books.

Richmond, A. (2008) Going beyond the magic number 7. *Psychology in the News*, 7 October.

Robbins, A. (1987) *Unlimited Power*. London: Simon & Schuster.

Roozendaal, B., McEwen, B.S. and Chattarji, S. (2009) Stress, memory and the amygdala. *Nature Reviews Neuroscience*, 10, June: 423–33.

Rose Charvet, S. (1997) *Words That Change Minds: Mastering the Language of Influence*, 2nd edn. Dubuque, IA: Kendall Hunt Publishing.

Rose Charvet, S. (2010) *The Customer Is Bothering Me*. Dubuque, IA: Kendall Hunt Publishing.

Roy, A.F. (2007) *An Examination of the Principle Based Leadership Trainings and Business Consultations of a Group Private Practice*. Boston: Massachusetts School of Professional Psychology.

Sample, I. (2007) Learn to forget: How the mind blocks painful memories. *Guardian*, 13 July.

Sedgeman, J. (2005) Health realization/innate health: Can a quiet mind and a positive feeling state be accessible over the lifespan without stress-relief techniques? *Medical Science Monitor*, 11(12): 47–52.

Senge, P.M., Kleiner, A., Roberts, C., Ross, R.B. and Smith, B.J. (1999) *The Fifth Discipline Fieldbook: Strategies and Tools for Building a Learning Organisation*. London: Nicholas Brealey Publishing.

Silvester, T. (2009) *Wordweaving*, vol. 1: *The Science of Suggestion*. Burwell, Cambs.: Quest Institute.

Singh, A. and Abraham, A. (2008) Neuro linguistic programming: A key to business excellence. *Total Quality Management*, 19(1–2), January–February: 139–47.

Sparrow, R.T. (2005) Authentic leadership and the narrative self. *Leadership Quarterly*, 16: 419–39.

Squirrel, L. (2009) Can neurolinguistic programming work with young children who display varying social, emotional and behavioural difficulties? *Current Research in NLP*, 1 (Proceedings of 2008 Conference): 109–20.

Sullivan, W. and Rees, J. (2009) *Clean Language: Revealing Metaphors and Opening Minds*. Bancyfelin, Carmarthen: Crown House Publishing.

Tosey, P. (2008) Neuro-linguistic programming: Learning and education – an introduction. *Encyclopaedia of Informal Education*, http:www.infed.org/biblio/nlp.htm/.

Tosey, P. and Mathison, J. (2009) *Neuro-Linguistic Programming: A Critical Appreciation for Managers and Developers*. Houndmills, Basingstoke: Palgrave Macmillan.

Wake, L. (2010) *NLP Principles in Practice*. St Albans: Ecademy Press.

Walker, L. (2004) *Changing with NLP: A Casebook of Neuro-Linguistic Programming in Medical Practice*. Milton Keynes: Radcliffe Medical Press.

Whitmore, J. (2010) *Coaching for Performance: Growing Human Potential and Purpose – The Principles and Practice of Coaching and Leadership*. London: Nicholas Brealey Publishing.

Youell, R. and Youell, C. (2011) *Effective NLP Skills: Creating Success*. London: Sunday Times/Kogan Page.

Yukl, G. (1998) *Leadership in Organisations*. Upper Saddle River, NJ: Prentice Hall.

Suggested
further reading

Alder, H. (1996) *NLP for Managers: How to Achieve Excellence at Work*. London: Piatkus.

Argyle, M. (1994) *The Psychology of Interpersonal Behaviour*. London: Penguin Books.

Bandler, R. and Grinder, J. (1975) *The Structure of Magic*, vol. I. Palo Alto, CA: Science and Behavior Books.

Bavister, S. and Vickers, A. (2004) *Essential NLP*. London: Teach Yourself.

Blanchard, K. (2007) *Leading at a Higher Level: Blanchard on How to Be a High Performing Leader*. Harlow: FT Prentice Hall.

Bradbury, A. (2010) *Develop Your NLP Skills*, 4th edn. London: Sunday Times/Kogan Page.

Brown, K. and Rutter, L. (2008) *Critical Thinking for Social Work*. Exeter: Learning Matters.

Goleman, D. (1998) *Working with Emotional Intelligence*. London: Bloomsbury Publishing.

Gray, I., Field, R. and Brown, K. (2010) *Effective Leadership, Management and Supervision in Health and Social Care*. Exeter: Learning Matters.

McDermott, I. and Jago, W. (2003) *The NLP Coach: A Comprehensive Guide to Personal Well-Being and Professional Success*. London: Piatkus.

O'Connor, J. (2001) *NLP Workbook: A Practical Guide to Achieving the Results You Want*. London: HarperCollins.

O'Connor, J. and Seymour, J. (2002) *Introducing NLP: Psychological Skills for Understanding and Influencing People*. London: Harper Element.

Rose Charvet, S. (1997) *Words That Change Minds: Mastering the Language of Influence*, 2nd edn. Dubuque, IA: Kendall Hunt Publishing.

Senge, P.M., Kleiner, A., Roberts, C., Ross, R.B. and Smith, B.J. (1999) *The Fifth Discipline Fieldbook: Strategies and Tools for Building a Learning Organisation*. London: Nicholas Brealey Publishing.

Wake, L. (2010) *NLP Principles in Practice*. St Albans: Ecademy Press.

Index